MEDIA-
WASTELAND OR
WONDERLAND

MEDIA-
WASTELAND OR WONDERLAND

OPPORTUNITIES AND DANGERS FOR
CHRISTIANS IN THE ELECTRONIC AGE

JOHN W. BACHMAN

Foreword by Martin E. Marty

AUGSBURG Publishing House • Minneapolis

MEDIA—WASTELAND OR WONDERLAND
Opportunities and Dangers for Christians in the Electronic Age

Scripture quotations unless otherwise noted are from the Revised Standard Version of the Bible, copyright 1946, 1952, and 1971 by the Division of Christian Education of the National Council of Churches.

Scripture quotations marked TEV are from The Good News Bible, Today's English Version, copyright 1966, 1971, 1976 by American Bible Society. Used by permission.

Library of Congress Cataloging in Publication Data

Bachman, John W.
  MEDIA—WASTELAND OR WONDERLAND.

  Bibliography: p.
  1. Mass media in religion.   I. Title.
BV652.95.B33 1985   260   84-24319
ISBN 0-8066-2116-8 (pbk.)

Manufactured in the U.S.A.   APH 10-4307

1 2 3 4 5 6 7 8 9 0 1 2 3 4 5 6 7 8 9

To
Beth
Sharon
John
Alison
lifetime participants
in an electronic culture

Contents

Foreword

Before live studio broadcasts begin, before the bright lights and cameras or microphones come on, someone appears on stage to warm up the audience. This person helps the audience become a community. She, or usually he, tries out a few weak jokes of the sort that will help the star attract spontaneous laughter because the audience will have shed inhibitions or been ready for something better. The warm-up person may give a bit of advice about when to applaud, how to behave, and what to watch for. Then as broadcast time approaches, the advance man takes his APPLAUD or SILENCE signs, his props, and his note cards offstage, recedes back into the darkness, watches the lights go on, and hopes for the best.

In many senses, people who write forewords for books serve comparable warm-up purposes in print media. If the broadcast that follows the warm-up is not worth paying attention to, the audience will be apathetic and listeners or viewers will twist dials. So a foreword writer cannot rescue a bad or even a weak book. Yet if the book has something to say, as I believe John W. Bachman's does, the pages up front can be of some service to readers. That service does not consist in holding up APPLAUD or SILENCE signs, or sticking them like little bookmarks in the pages which follow. Nor is one likely to serve or to upstage an author like Bachman with attempts to outdo him on the points he makes, or, on the other hand, to say, "This is not a very strong point, so let me help it along." He does not need help.

Instead a foreword writer, or at least this one, conceives of the task on lines like this: readers who buy (one hopes), borrow, read, and use a book on a particular subject bring some expectations and hopes to it. They cannot be expected to have read all the previous literature or to have devoted a big part of their lives to reflecting on the problems it takes up. If they did, they would less likely get the new book; they would be sated or bored and would "turn it off" in advance. The foreword writer is someone who has read long and widely in the field and has reflected on the subject enough to help locate the book and its issues—without having enough expertise or energy to have written the book itself. From that middle-range vantage such a foreword person can be a signaler, a taker of temperatures, a planter of signposts, a pointer to significances. Let me try.

This book has at least three main purposes. First, it is important for all of us to locate ourselves in our time and place. "Whoever named the water, it certainly wasn't the fish." The fish was enveloped by and dependent upon the water, which was so close to it that there was difficulty knowing that water was a strange environment. We are enveloped by the atmosphere and milieu of our culture, and while we have been given intelligences denied the fish—while having been denied some of their equipment for coping and their skills—we still have difficulty assessing the meanings of our time and place.

Call in the experts. John W. Bachman is not setting out to be a philosopher of history with answers to all problems. He is, however, a veteran and accomplished Christian reflector on mass media and has taken pains to sort out information and opinions that will help others know what is going on. I recall a cartoon of a militant and at the same time befuddled dowager marching with a sign that said, "Will somebody please tell me what the hell is going on?" John Bachman helps tell what in, or of, or about hell is going on in the culture and what in heaven's name or from heaven Christians might do to understand and change it. He helps bring information together and puts names on complexities. That is therapeutic and helpful for purposes of Christian action.

Second, Bachman is a good sorter. People speak of information overloads, yet it is still possible for people who live surrounded by media to be "underloaded." That is, we do not naturally have the information we need in order to make up our minds. Or, if we have information, we may not have taken pains to sort it. Bachman brings it together, sorts it, and presents it in ordered ways. He is not a mere sorter, however, but a good one. For me this means that he is balanced, judicious, critical, and capable of teaching.

There are two ways to write books on this subject and have them immediately located. One can write a total denunciation, issue a big blast, demolish everything in the world of media, in the interest of taste or faith. From the viewpoint of Christian faith, of course all things human have to be seen in and under the mark of death, finitude, failure, or folly. Demolition is an easy task, but not a helpful one. Or one can write a "puff," a simple upbeat and sunny defense of the world as it is. On those terms, some Christian communicators have oversold the media as if they would not only help announce the kingdom of God but be the kingdom. Such books can appeal to dreams and fantasies, and will attract wide notice from dreamers and fantasists. Yet since they do not replicate the real world or address it in terms of a faith centered in the cross, they are creators of illusions or lies.

Bachman has taken a third way. His way will not produce headlines or, probably, best-sellers, because it deals with the ambiguity of life, the double-sidedness of human creativity. He knows that radio, cinema, television, and the newer computer-related technologies can be used "demonically," but they need not be. They can serve humane and evangelical purposes. He knows that they have enormous influence for good, when properly used. Yet he knows why ordinarily they will not be so used. This is not a wishy-washy "on one hand" or "on the other hand" book, but one which shows something of what can work for God's purposes despite finitude and what can work against them despite claims that the pious are using these media to good effect.

Third, this book has some implied "how to" dimensions. Bachman is not interested in helping create new audiences for media as such, or to turn people so that they will turn off electronic devices. He is helping provide a kind of "do it yourself" kit so that Christians can interpret and intervene in a world that so often seems beyond the range of understanding, beyond a zone in which they can have effect.

The book is not designed essentially for the .002% of the Christian world that is directly involved in programming, but in that much, much larger percentage of Christians who make use of the media and sometimes wish that Christian themes, approaches, and content had a larger and more effective place. He is a bit more hopeful than I about the uses that mainline Christians can discover when it comes to media. By mainline, here, I mean those Christians for whom media presentations are expressions of bodies of Christians, the church or churches, and not sensationalist extensions of charismatic individuals and their empires. At the same time, this book will help steer such thoughtful Christians away from what would be futile experiments.

Most important, he contributes to the understanding that the Christian world has to help create critical audiences for secular media and expectant audiences for experimental Christian media. To assert that they should generate such audiences is easy. To begin to show why and how to go about that demands expertise and energy. In other words, warm-up time is over, its duller lights are going down, my page-equivalent-to-a-microphone will lose its place and power, and it is time to get at the main act. John, you're on your own! And so, dear readers, are you . . . .

Martin E. Marty
The University of Chicago

Preface

Revolution or Counterrevolution?

"There's always a media revolution going on, and it's getting to be a nuisance," wrote Michael Strange in *New York Magazine*. Some nuisances, however, are more important than others. To some people Hitler was a nuisance. Steam engines were nuisances to persons who didn't operate them. Today's nuisance may be tomorrow's threat or marvel.

Human history occasionally changes direction because of a discovery. This has happened with the wheel, fire, gunpowder, and the printing press. The automobile is credited with (or blamed for) a range of developments in family life and urban sprawl. The industrial revolution, after inundating the North and West, is sweeping its tide of gains and losses over the so-called developing world.

More recently western civilization has entered a new stage: the information age, growing out of a communications revolution. I prefer to call it the electronic age, to take into account all of the new developments from radio and television to cable and satellites, videodisc and videotape, teletext and videotext, computers, and you name it.

Electronic media already are very influential. American children average 26 hours per week in front of the lighted tube. Senior citizens have spent the equivalent of eight continuous years watching television. Respondents to a *U.S. News and World Report* survey on "Who Runs America?" placed television second only to the White House, and ahead of big business, the Supreme Court, the U.S. Senate, labor unions, and Wall Street. Organized religion was rated no. 28, followed only by small business and cinema. The newest electronic technologies, combining all the possibilities of earlier ones, are expected by some experts to transform the economy, education, entertainment, politics, and leisure.

The prospects for such a wonderland are not enough, in the minds of some people, to revise Newton Minow's description of television as a "vast wasteland." For Christians there is little basis for optimism in the present ethical climate, whether that climate is affected by the mass media or only reflected in them. In one survey of Lutheran families, more than 93% of the persons responding said they were less than completely satisfied with the quality of television today.

Gathered communities of Christians have had little impact on the media. Some denominations and individual evangelists have invested substantially in programs with varying results. Most churches, however, have participated in broadcasting in only a limited way and have been even less active in influencing media policies. Entering the electronic age, organized religion does not appear prepared to rise above its 28th place in offering direction for national policies.

This need not be the case. The church enjoys the respect and trust of many citizens. In a nationwide Gallup poll conducted every year for a decade, the church and organized religion have received higher votes of confidence than public schools, the Supreme Court, newspapers, and Congress. The confidence margin over television has been two to one, with big business rated even lower. We as Christians could exert more influence if we were better informed and took more responsibility. What should be done *with* broadcasting and the newer technological developments? What should be done *about* them? This is the time to ask such questions, instead of treating electronic capabilities as science fiction until other interests have monopolized them for their own practical purposes.

The newer media may be used simply to complete the revolution anticipated in George Orwell's *1984*—making persons into objects of machines, manipulated by powerful, monopolistic forces. Individuals can be overwhelmed by complex data and a barrage of sensations. On the other hand, some of the current developments can help to counteract authoritarian tendencies: instead of being limited to three similar networks a person may select from 60 television channels plus access by computer to the resources of libraries and art galleries. Opportunities for response and interaction are also multiplied.

Walter Cronkite, retired high priest of network news, has said of the communications revolution, "We may now be in for a counterrevolution that can help revive a sense of the local, the neighborhood. . . . "

Whether it is called revolution, counterrevolution or reformation, Christians have a task to perform in responding to the electronic age. This task will require more thought than most people devote to the "boob tube." Peggy Charren, founder and president of Action for Children's Television, has said, "We take television for granted because it's in our living room and we don't think it will do any harm the way we'd worry about a stranger coming in and talking to our child." The newer forms of television, along with video games and computers, will open our homes to a host of strangers.

In the following pages we will suggest how to deal with these visitors. We will sift through dreams and warnings about the new age, and then indicate how we as Christians may face the future without illusion or despair.

In one sense this book attempts the impossible. The situation described changes so rapidly that some paragraphs are bound to be outdated before they appear in print. Almost every newspaper and magazine I have read and every hour spent watching television has yielded material inviting additions or revisions in the manuscript. All predictions in this area are precarious. Critics could claim that it is too soon to reach such conclusions as I submit in the final chapters. I would maintain instead that, unless the public is alerted immediately to what is happening, it will be too late to enlist a powerful force in the enlightenment of society.

This book is not addressed primarily to media specialists, most of whom share my concerns. It is directed to "ordinary people," especially Christians whose only contacts with telecommunications are casual but whose values and sense of social responsibility are challenged by current developments in the media. I have tried, therefore, to include elements from technology, theology, and communication theory without resorting to the jargon of those fields.

In this effort I have been assisted by the National Council of Churches' Dave Pomeroy, who checked the manuscript for technical accuracy; by our sons Charles, church executive, and John, TV anchorman, who made many thoughtful suggestions; and by the editors of Augsburg Publishing House, who have been encouraging and receptive. As always, my wife Elsie has prepared the drafts for submission, proofreading and correcting in the process. She is also the first subject for my informal research into how readers are likely to respond to a paragraph or chapter. I am grateful for all of the time and effort contributed by friends and family.

PART ONE

Between Wasteland and Wonderland

The Look through Dark Glasses

A former advertising executive, Jerry Mander, has published the book *Four Arguments for the Elimination of Television*. Another author, Marie Wynn, argues in *The Plug-In Drug* that the only way to deal with television is to stop watching it.

Is TV so terrible? And are the newer electronic developments likely to make things worse?

Personal morality

The most common accusations against the media focus on their alleged preoccupation with sex and violence. There is no doubt that viewers are exposed to a picture of life at odds with traditional personal morality. British marriage counselors have voiced their unhappiness with the "Dallas" series, imported from the U.S. Stephen Saunders of the Marriage Guidance Center said, "In 'Dallas' the answer to marital problems is either to jump in bed with someone else, sock your partner on the jaw, or shoot someone." Irene Watson, head of the National Housewives Association, said, "They treat marriage like a secondhand car market. When they get fed up with one model, they trade it in for a new one."

Whether the media have brought about changes or whether they are simply reflecting them is a question to which we will return periodically. One thing is certain: whatever is portrayed in the public media, and often reported as the behavior of celebrities, is certified to many viewers as being acceptable.

A fan magazine reports that actor Lionel Stander "strongly believes in marriages—he has had six of them." Johnny Carson is one of the most talented performers on the air but he may also, unintentionally, be the biggest drug pusher in the country because of his repetitious, jovial references to drug use by band members. The humorous treatment of his own sequential polygamy is also a part of the climate in which older values are ridiculed.

In his novel *The Laughing Man* Tom T. Hall warns that modern media, under their entertaining exterior, are really conveying serious messages. He describes his book as a protest "about the way the media is [sic] trying to change your morals." One conclusion is inevitable: the social changes of the 60s have been expedited and exported from New York and Los Angeles to the rest of the country.

The extension of cable TV and the proliferation of videotapes and video games have opened a new market for exploitative sex. Perhaps it is more accurate to say that an existing market has been expanded. Magazines such as *Hustler* and *Penthouse*, along with many of the newsstand paperbacks, demonstrate that print has not overlooked the "new morality."

Violence

There is no end to the argument—and the research—over the influence of media violence. The quantity of violence in television has been documented: children and other viewers are exposed to a fantastic number of fistfights, shootings, stabbings, and general mayhem. Modern media, of course, are not the only ones to include violence; Shakespeare, the Bible, and traditional fairy tales have their share. Electronic media, however, may provide a more intense experience and video games even offer the opportunity to participate vicariously in slaughter.

The direct, immediate effect of sensational episodes on a few unstable viewers may be obvious, but longer-range influences on the wider audience are difficult to measure, at least with present instruments. Different people respond in different ways, partly because we are all subject to such a range of stimuli that it is difficult to isolate the effect of a single medium.

It is possible to quote research producing contradictory evidence. Most social scientists are therefore cautious in their analyses, as seen in the report by members of the Presidential Commission on the Causes and Prevention of Violence. One of their early conclusions says only, "The weight of social science stands in opposition to the conclusion that mass media portrayals of violence have no effect upon individuals, groups, and society." In accompanying exposition they are less restrained and assert the "probability" that such portrayals are "one major contributing factor" in explaining violent behavior in America today.

Other studies go further. One by the National Institute of Mental Health states that there is "overwhelming evidence that excessive violence in television causes aggressive behavior in children." A report from the Surgeon General's Office was very specific: "The causal relationship between televised violence and anti-social behavior is sufficient to warrant appropriate and immediate remedial action."

Questions remain. How much violence is "excessive"? Are there significant differences in the kinds of violence presented? What about the context in which violence occurs? Is all "aggressive behavior" bad? In later chapters we will be exploring such issues, along with suggestions for "appropriate remedial action." For now we will only observe that there has been little such action, which may not be surprising when we remember that the Surgeon General has presented more concrete evidence for the hazards of tobacco, with only limited effect on the smoking of cigarettes.

Sensationalism

Creators of programs for the mass media can claim that the emphasis on sex and violence is not intended to corrupt listener-viewers, but is only an attempt to attract and hold their attention. In the face of cutthroat competition for audiences, producers resort to higher and higher levels of sensation. One writer mused, "today's sensation is tomorrow's ho hum." A magazine editor said plaintively, "We can no longer sell pornography; we must sell tastelessness."

One of the nation's largest advertising agencies, the J. Walter Thompson Company, made a presentation several years ago to its commercial colleagues and competitors on "The Desensitization of America." A host of striking examples was assembled to support the claim that the advertising and entertainment industries are escalating the level of sensationalism to the point where results can be damaging both to society and to the industry.

Advocates for causes, even peaceful ones, have discovered that their best opportunity to gain access to the media is to stage confrontations. Terrorists hijack planes, take hostages, and bomb buildings, knowing that the result will be an airing of their claims, no matter how outrageous.

Even respected journalists somtimes go overboard to exploit sensationalism for ratings. The CBS program "60 Minutes" did a hatchet job on the National Council of Churches and the World Council of Churches despite abundant, easily available evidence disproving the program's deceptive inferences. Selective interviews and editing can be used to excite and fascinate viewers while distorting truth.

Since conflict is sensational, the media tend to underline or even create adversarial relationships. There is always the desire to identify the good guys and the bad guys, leading to oversimplification. Bad news is assumed to attract more attention than good news. Writer Norman Cousins contends that the disaster-prone tendency of the media "leads to a public mood of defeatism and despair, which in themselves tend to be inhibitors of progress." He adds: "An unrelieved diet of eruptive news depletes the essential energies a free society needs. A mood of hopelessness and cynicism is hardly likely to furnish the energy needed to meet serious challenges."

Oversimplification

Walter Cronkite, addressing the Radio and TV News Directors' Association, once said, "I'm afraid we compress so well as to almost defy the viewer and listener to understand what we say. We now have a communication problem of immense dimensions partly of our own making." Most people turn to television for most of their news but the time devoted to such programs allows for only very limited coverage of events—scarcely more than headlines.

The United States political process has been affected by this tendency to oversimplify. Campaign money is concentrated on spot announcements which focus on image rather than substance, avoiding controversial issues. The ads follow polls rather than lead the constituency. In 1982 nearly all congressional candidates had spots pledging no change in Social Security although all knew that a change was necessary. Advertising executive David Altman has said that he would favor prohibiting the use of 30- and 60-second spots in political campaigns. "Political spots do not tell anything about candidates," he said, and added, "They are cinematographic seductions. That's why we continually elect candidates who later 'surprise' us."

There is an understandable tendency on the part of government officials to stage events, even on the international scene, which will allow the media to report them as wins rather than losses.

There is hope, as I will be reporting in the next chapter, that the newer media will break out of this time bind and encourage reflective thinking on complex and controversial issues. Whether or not citizens conditioned to form opinions on the basis of 30-second blurbs will take the time to become better informed is a crucial question.

Materialism

"America is growing great by the systematic creation of discontent," claimed one advertising executive. In both programs and spot announcements, commercial broadcasting extols the acquisition of things. Manufacturers play on every conceivable human desire and weakness to sell products. For every fear or feeling of insecurity there is a new, improved soap, toothpaste, or lotion to make the user feel charming and irresistible. If life is less than perfect, the right automobile or even soft drink will give you new zest for living. A drug containing new, fast-acting ingredients will cure whatever ails you. In an age of anxiety there's nothing like a shopping spree for consolation.

For the Christian this not only conflicts with concepts of stewardship but raises questions about false gods. Is advertising making puppets out of people? Buddy Scott, vice-president and manager of TM Productions in Dallas says, "Advertising can be magical. It has the power to alter our perception and our thinking, stimulating desire and changing lives—unobtrusively, unconsciously, and almost insidiously."

More and more ads are being aired on American television as both government regulation and industry codes lose influence. Cable and pay-TV were once seen as correctives for excessive commercialism, but there is no guarantee that they will be free of advertising.

Critics wearing the darkest of glasses even blame the artificially stimulated marketing campaigns of the mass media for the squandering of our natural resources, with accompanying pollution and poisonous wastes.

One economic effect more clearly traceable to the media is the disproportionate salary scale prevalent in the United States. Celebrities either from the media or created by the media, as in sports, command salaries out of line with their contribution to the public welfare. The effects of these warped standards on other industries and, eventually, on inflation, are at least cause for speculation.

Depersonalization

Advertising may be not only materialistic but outrageously tasteless. One dinnertime news program was interrupted by ads for indigestion relief, a toilet bowl cleaner, and a hemorrhoid ointment. But it is not only in advertising that the media tend to exploit persons. Game shows make willing freaks out of covetous participants. Insensitive reporters poke microphones in front of people shattered by catastrophe, asking, "How do you feel?" One such interviewer was so ill-prepared that he could only ask a man just declared innocent of murder, "Are you glad it's over?"

Television and films are notorious for their stereotyping according to race, sex, and occupation. In recent years there have been attempts to portray black families in situation comedies, but even the producers of those programs cannot resist the temptation to stereotype in a denigrating way. In the "Good Times" series, for example, the family was molded into a fatherless welfare situation and Esther Rolle, who played the mother, resigned out of frustration over the characterization of the older son, J. J. (played by Jimmy Walker). She explained:

> I just couldn't go on any longer with that kind of outrageous character as the role model for black children . . . he didn't work, he cut school, he was disrespectful.

When she told executives her intention to resign, she was warned that this could jeopardize chances for being cast in future productions, but she took her stand anyway. She has been offered little television work since then.

Fathers are portrayed regularly as amiable nitwits. Perhaps this is only an appropriate corrective for the other sexist image of men as dynamic, domineering achievers. Only recently has the attempt begun to correct the stereotyping of women in subservient roles.

Cerebral bypass

Not all dangers from media exposure are as obvious as the ones identified so far. The most serious threats from cathode ray tube watching may be more subtle and less recognized. One threat that I label as "cerebral bypass" combines features described by others as escapism, the narcotic function, fragmentation, and cognitive impairment. In simpler language it can be claimed that the most popular electronic media discourage thinking.

Television has been described as the electronic fireplace of our time—absorbing and hypnotic, inviting trancelike watching. One psychoanalyst has said, "The television medium is practically devoid of interpretive demands upon the viewer" and "affords the most convenient relaxation of the sense of reality." A related criticism maintains that there is no other childhood experience that permits quite so much intake while demanding so little outflow. It is said to be similar to daydreaming but with outside input to the dreams.

How can so much action and excitement be so tranquilizing? Evidently this happens partly because of the fragmentation; not only news but all programs are broken down into brief segments, anticipating rapid changes, leading to a shortened attention span and lack of reflectiveness. Even the educational attempt "Sesame Street" switches rapidly from one item to another. Many elementary teachers are reporting that their TV-conditioned pupils have difficulty concentrating for a reasonable length of time; learning is retarded.

Episcopalian communication officer Robert W. Morse has offered an explanation: television does not allow a person to think at a comfortable pace; unlike a reader, the television viewer cannot look back to previous paragraphs to compare and test ideas; mental "talking back" is therefore stifled. He goes so far as to conclude: "The very act of watching is harmful to the cognitive development of children and affects adversely the moral, social, emotional and religious development as a consequence." He adds that television "debilitates an important cognitive function in adults, the one that permits abstract reasoning—and hence related capacities for moral decision-making, learning, religious growth, and psychological individualization." Morse is describing a process of brainwashing or cerebral bypass.

There is some support for his theory from research. Experiments in different centers have indicated that brain wave activity generally slows with watching TV, regardless of the program being viewed. The result is a predominently alpha state, with viewers being "spaced out." This finding helps me to understand why I can fall asleep watching football on Sunday afternoon.

Not all viewers, of course, respond to all programs in this way. And television is not the only communication medium demonstrating difficulty in stimulating the brain. Preachers have known this problem; even Paul put Eutychus to sleep.

The electronic media, however, seem to have a special capability. They can bypass the brain, not by being boring, but by bombarding people with exciting sensations. The enormous investment of time and money in video games seems to support this theory. Thoughtful observers fear that the result of indiscriminate media exposure is not merely escapism but addiction, a condition which retards the development of humans created in the image of God.

Unreliable guide

A majority of adults and nearly as high a percentage of children use television to learn how to handle specific life problems. This conclusion was reached by social scientists preparing a report for the Surgeon General's Advisory Committee on Television and Social Behavior.

250,000 letters, mostly requests for medical advice, were sent to Marcus Welby, M.D., during the first five years of his TV practice. Later, of course, the image was exploited for the sale of products.

All art may distort life for its purposes, but television, with its action and immediacy, appears to be so real that many viewers expect life to imitate it. A classic cartoon pictured two youngsters in the windows of a parked auto, sorrowfully watching their dad repairing a tire in a downpour. The harassed father was remonstrating, "Don't you understand? This is *life*, this is what is happening. We can't switch to another channel." One study calculated that 58% of shots fired on television miss their target, giving a false impression of the use of firearms.

Even on a surface level, the perpetual drinking and smoking in entertainment programs creates a questionable portrayal of reality. Soap operas, acknowledged as presenting role models for many daytime viewers, treat the absence of inhibitions as routine behavior. The weekly review of soap opera plots published for the sake of addicts who have missed seeing episodes, has no resemblance to a diary of real life. Here is a typical summary of one week on a series:

> A torn Grant gets drunk at a Labor Day party and begs Celia to help him. Grant discovers that Prof. Jerrold has set up a trust fund for Grant and Celia's first child and that Grant is the sole heir. Gregory manages to get Grant to try and get a disc from Prof. Jerrold. Professor is stunned as Grant holds a gun on him. Grant realizes he cannot shoot the professor. As he lowers the gun, a shot rings out and the professor dies. Rose and Jake make love. When Lu comes on to him, Blackie backs off, telling her he's not certain of his feelings. Bobbi intends to move in with Brock as soon as he tells his daughter about their planned arrangements. Brian is named Lee's new campaign manager.

Programs which once avoided serious issues now are more likely to exploit them. A 1984 episode of "Buffalo Bill" dealing with abortion lost no opportunity for humor but avoided all questions of personal responsibility, honesty, and morality. Significantly, the program stimulated only 4 telephone calls to NBC while an episode of "Maude" 11 years earlier, also involving abortion, resulted in 1500 calls to CBS. Divorce, cancer, homosexuality, racism—all are used to develop dramatic plots without reference to basic religious values.

A special concern is the effect of such apparent realism on children. Psychologist David Elkind claims that the result is "pseudo sophistication, children knowing more than they can understand." He lumps modern "children's books" with TV and says, "making experiences more accessible does not make them more comprehensible."

Media myths

The total impact of popular media is undoubtedly more than the sum of its individual scenes. Certain myths are so pervasive that they must make a cumulative impression on listener-viewers. I will call attention to only a few of the more common ones.

1. Look out for no. 1. Whether in "Dallas," "The A-Team," "Monday Night Football," "As the World Turns," or Pac-Man,

the fittest survive through force and aggression. The only worthwhile goal is to become no. 1.

2. Selfishly pursue happiness. There are no ground rules in the search for enjoyment. Everything that brings pleasure is good and for sale at some price.

3. Reverence is irrelevant. Outside of humorous or superficial references to church and clergy, nearly all characters in the modern media are drawn to act as though religious faith has no relationship to daily decisions and actions. God is even more remote than outer space and the future has no relation to the present.

4. Change is beautiful. Whatever is new is better than the old. Science and industry create marvelous improvements in our way of life. Adherence to traditional moral standards is unattractive and pathetic because it resists change.

5. Trust in original goodness. Underneath the unpleasant qualities all humans are basically good. We only need openness and honesty to achieve a peaceful, just world.

New hazards from new technologies

With new electronic developments come new threats to individuals and society.

Two-way systems like Qube in Columbus, Ohio, allow cable TV viewers to react to programs. They may express approval or disapproval, register votes after a debate, or order a product advertised. Such an arrangement, however, creates an opportunity for invasion of privacy. Central computers can record all responses and develop a profile of each subscriber, charting preferences and convictions. Advertisers and politicians covet access to such information. Home computers, connected by telephone to central information sources, also offer the possibility of developing a significant data bank about the persons using the instruments. Government agencies are capable of intercepting computerized messages as they pass through U.S. communication channels.

There have been well-publicized instances where amateurs were able to crack computer codes, breaking a system's confidentiality. Anyone with a pressing desire for personal information about another may be tempted. Carl Bernstein, *Washington Post* reporter who helped to expose Watergate, has written that once, in the course of his investigation, he traced telephone calls to G. Gordon Liddy with the help of sources in the Bell system. He admitted that he would have been outraged if subjected to a similar inquiry, but he went ahead anyway and got a list of the calls.

Criminals can infiltrate computer systems to steal money or data or to sabotage a company's operations. Improperly programmed electronic medical instruments have resulted in wrong diagnoses and at least one death.

In 1979 a computer contributed to the deaths of 257 people. After a jetliner crashed into a mountain in Antarctica, killing all on board, an investigatory commission concluded that a major cause was the fact that the computerized flight plan fed into the aircraft's automatic pilot had been changed without the pilot's knowledge.

Two frightening incidents occurred in 1979 and 1980 when national defense computers erroneously reported that the United States was under attack and the armed forces were put on alert. In each case the error was discovered within minutes.

The sheer volume of accessible information in the electronic age may be disquieting to individuals. Will all of society's problems appear to be too difficult to face? If so, despair or apathy may result. On the other hand, we will have to guard against the illusion that all answers are available by pushing the right buttons. David Burnham, *New York Times* reporter, in his book *The Rise of the Computer State* says, "Society requires more than calculation; it requires intuition and wisdom."

As we shall comment later, precautions can be taken against some of the emerging threats from new technologies, but one result, increased unemployment, is causing immediate hardship.

The movement to automation and use of robots is inevitable. At Inland Steel one operation which used to take 5 days now requires 10 minutes. A General Electric plant that builds locomotives needs 16 hours for a process previously running 16 days.

Italian Fiat believes sensory robots will slash manpower requirements 90% over 10 years. In Japan 50 robots are replacing themselves at the rate of 24 per day. In industry after industry machines are replacing humans.

Villain or scapegoat

This chapter has reviewed an imposing list of accusations leveled against modern electronic means of communication. Television and computers can be made to sound especially villainous. It is possible that some of these criticisms reflect the desire to find a convenient scapegoat to blame for all sorts of evils, allowing the real culprits to shirk responsibility. Certainly the electronic media have contributions to make to individual and corporate life. It is time to explore those positive factors before considering how to deal with the new technologies.

A Rose-colored 2
View

Modern media enthusiasts anticipate the coming of the "global village," the human community enlightened by information and stimulation from all over the world. Not even desert nomads or remote mountaineers will be isolated from the traffic in ideas. A postliterate culture will feature involvement, empathy, and wholeness. Democracy will thrive because everyone can participate in decision making. Cross-cultural understanding will promote peace.

The electronic media can make possible common, collective experiences which tend to unite populations. Americans remember the Kennedy funeral, the first moon landing, the Olympic hockey victory, and the release of the Iran hostages.

Even in its present form television has its intellectual defenders. The philosopher Mortimer J. Adler, who for more than 50 years has been a proponent of mental exercise, regards television as an appropriate educational medium. When print-oriented colleagues look down their noses at the tube, Adler responds: "Look, I think nine-tenths of the 40,000 books published every year are crap. . . . Television hasn't got a worse record than that." He explains that the publishing industry makes a social and educational contribution by the relatively few good books released annually, and claims that there are a few good television programs each year too. "Sure, most of the stuff is tawdry, vulgar, trivial," he admits, but adds: "So? Think of the paperbacks in the grocery store, the drugstore. Lousy! They're just as mind-killing as the bad TV."

There are students of the media who claim, based on limited research, that it is primarily "media snobs" who are upset by the low caliber of most prime-time television. Sociologist Herbert Gans, in his book *Popular and High Culture*, says, "Pap is an annoyance and hazard only to those who take it seriously—which, perhaps significantly, seldom includes those who enjoy it."

Entertainment value

The popular media do not deserve condemnation simply because they offer so much entertainment. Anyone who has been confined to bed for a period of time (as well as pastors who visit shut-ins regularly) recognizes the restorative function performed by radio and television. Laborers performing repetitive, boring tasks for eight hours daily and professionals at home after a day of making complex decisions want and need relaxation and even diversion.

Actual medical studies, done separately at Stanford University and the University of California, show that programs like television situation comedies can have amazing health benefits. Prof. William F. Fry Jr. concluded, "By watching shows that make you laugh, and avoiding shows full of violence, you can clearly add years to your life." The research indicated that watching comedy shows, soap operas, musical variety shows, and even cartoons can reduce harmful stress, relax muscles, stimulate the heart and respiratory system, and improve circulation.

Dan Wakefield, journalist and novelist, has recounted how he, "as an innocent intellectual," had no understanding of television soap operas until he started watching daytime TV in a time of crisis. He wrote, "I think that if for nothing else I will always love daytime television soap operas for being the only medium that offered me solace during that dreary post-divorce holiday season. . . . I watched one soap opera after another, and was relieved to find the lives of perfectly nice people portrayed who were not all rosy-cheeked with fa-la-la-de-da, but who had troubles, confusions and traumas whose pain and intensity were heightened by the pressure of the holidays."

Other journalists were amazed to discover that students in colleges and universities in the 70s were devoting so much time to watching soap operas, especially "All My Children." Classroom schedules were planned around it. Television sets in every fraternity, sorority, dormitory, and student union were tuned to it. Two out of three students were reported to be familiar with the plot.

Even game shows have their defenders, not surprisingly from within the industry. Mark Goodson, who has produced "What's My Line?," "To Tell the Truth," "Password," "Concentration," "Now You See It," "The Price Is Right," "Match Game," "Family Feud," and "Tattletales," explains: "There are two types of drama, the type that is written and done with actors for laughs or suspense, and the type that allows you to sit at home and watch actual people involved in actual situations with actual emotions and you can say, 'I could be there myself.' These dramas are unwritten and the endings cannot be planned. That is the drama of actuality, and that is all a game show is about." Not all game shows are identical; there is a great difference, for example, between the relatively low-key "Wheel of Fortune" and the frenzied "Family Feud." Shows featuring celebrities as contestants are still a different type.

To the accusation that contestants are manipulated, Chuck Barris, producer of "The Newlywed Game," "The Dating Game," and "The New Treasure Hunt," responds that they want to be manipulated. He says, "They've watched the show for years. They know what's going on. And in 90 percent of the cases, they're going to leave saying they had a good time. . . . They don't find it humiliating. They find it exhilarating, considering where they're coming from. They're coming from a drab existence."

Barris has referred to himself as "the King of Slob Culture," but before his insights are discredited on this basis it may be wise to recall the character of Sabina from Thornton Wilder's *Skin of Our Teeth*. While George and Maggie Antrobus are thinking about how they are going to begin life anew after war's terrible destruction, the seductress and working girl Sabina wants only to go to the movies. She says, "I'm just an ordinary girl. . . . But you're a bright man . . . and of course you've invented the alphabet and the wheel . . . and if you've got any other plans, my God, don't let me upset them. Only every now and then I've got to go to the movies. I mean, my nerves can't stand it."

Sitcoms, soap operas, and game shows may not provide the most therapeutic form of diversion, but until educators or clergy can offer better alternatives, millions will turn for solace to what is now available on the tube.

News

The popular media are capable of providing more than entertainment, with news as the best example. Whatever the validity of abundant criticisms, television is regarded by most Americans as not only their primary but their most credible source of news. According to a Roper study 40% of Americans get *all* of their news from television. Since broadcast journalists report what has been called "history on the run," it may be unfair to expect the nightly newscasts to reflect an analytical perspective.

By use of graphics, maps, charts, and symbols television can help viewers understand unfamiliar material. Working journalists in all media take pride in a dedication to accuracy and freedom that often transcends the political orientation of both industry ownership and government officials. This Anglo-American tradition was observed during the Falklands War when Prime Minister Margaret Thatcher attacked British radio and television coverage for being evenhanded. She told Parliament, "I understand that there are times when we and the Argentines are almost being treated as equals." U.S. TV news undoubtedly contributed to support for the civil rights movement and opposition to the Vietnam War.

Documentary specials on both commercial and public networks provide in-depth coverage of events and issues treated only briefly in regular newscasts. The PBS series "Vietnam: A Television History" was a significant probe into a national trauma. "A Walk through the 20th Century with Bill Moyers" offered a fascinating look into the history of this era.

Networks and local stations are increasing both time and money invested in news. Independent Network News and the Public Broadcasting System devote a full hour to evening news. In some markets both cable and over-the-air stations extend this to a two-hour block. In radio there are all-news stations. Young journalists today may aspire to operate a cable news channel, much like their predecessors looked forward to owning a community newspaper.

Education and public service

Commercial broadcasting also engages in public service. Devoting spot announcements to this purpose probably accomplishes little, because spots are useful mainly for brand name identification and depend upon saturation and audience receptivity for their effectiveness. Presidential addresses and special coverage of critical events do make an impression. Fund-raising extravaganzas such as the Muscular Distrophy Telethon support research and benevolent causes. Incidental features of entertainment programs occasionally accomplish something worthwhile. When the Fonz got a library card, thousands of young people applied for their own. When Starsky and Hutch used seatbelts, it is claimed that large numbers followed their example.

Writers and producers of prime time programs sometimes attempt deliberately to influence opinions. In "Kill Me If You Can," the story of Caryl Chessman's 12 years on San Quentin's death row, producer Buzz Kulik admitted that the point of view was clearly anti-capital punishment.

The NBC docu-drama "Case of Rape" reached a 58% audience share in illuminating inequities in rape laws. Its writer, Robert Thompson, has claimed that his program "literally changed the law in America."

More formal learning is made possible through schools and universities of the air. A few children's programs attempt to influence positively. Research has indicated that exposure to "Mr. Roger's Neighborhood" made children three to five years old more cooperative. After extensive use of "The Electric Company" series in an Ohio elementary school for one year, third-graders scored five months higher in vocabulary than comparative scores of third graders the year before.

There are now nearly 300 public television stations in the United States, with the system providing signals that are viewable in more than 80% of the nation's homes. Despite cutbacks in national funding, the breadth and quality of programs has increased, attracting larger audiences. A single opera performance televised live from Lincoln Center in New York is viewed by an audience that would otherwise require 2500 sold-out performances of the Metropolitan Opera.

More diversity

It cannot be denied that educational and public service programs are an exception in commercial television, the dominant public medium. All three networks struggle for the largest possible audience by filling their schedules with entertainment programs assembled to fit the "lowest common denominator." But this situation has already been modified in radio. With the multiplication of FM outlets, especially in the larger markets, there are stations catering to all sorts of minority tastes. The Federal Communications Commission has decided to allow 125 new unlimited time AM stations to be licensed and more FM stations may also be authorized.

The new technologies may affect television in a similar way, a prospect to be explored in Chapter 4. Already there are indications of things to come. As many as 8000 low-power TV stations may be approved for operation over a limited radius. Already cable viewing is reducing the total size of the three-network audience.

Cable television originated simply as a means of bringing clearer TV reception by wire to homes where over-the-air signals were hampered by distance, mountains, or tall buildings. More recently, however, it has become the source of many more program services than are available from standard transmitting stations. Movies and sports dominate the schedules, but there can also be features for special audiences too small to justify network attention.

C-SPAN, one channel on the basic service of most cable systems, carries gavel to gavel coverage of the U.S. House of Representatives. Another national channel, Warner Amex's Nickelodeon, carries programs for young people 13 hours a day for 7 days, serving all ages from preschool through teens.

When children participate in producing cable programs, the process of scripting, shooting, and editing is demystifying. Critical judgment is stimulated and imaginations are put to work, counteracting the passivity engendered by overexposure to TV.

In Sun Prairie, Wisconsin, a local children's channel was mandated by city ordinance. KDS-4 is staffed by children aged 8 to 13, creating and producing a wide range of programs. They have even staged a satellite interconnect between American children and children in Australia.

Less exotic instruments are video disc and video cassette recorders (VCRs). Cassette machines, especially, are being purchased by the millions and offer the possibility of selective viewing by allowing owners to record preferred programs whenever transmitted and then to see them when convenient. Prerecorded cassettes are readily available from rental agencies and many public libraries. VCRs also facilitate local production for specialized audiences.

Demassified media

Alvin Toffler in *The Third Wave* anticipates the coming of "demassified media," electronic instruments not only used to transmit standardized programs to millions of passive recipients, but offering opportunities for personal selection, response, and interaction.

Videotex (or videotext) employs the telephone and a modified TV set, with keyboard or keypad, to connect with one or more computers storing information and graphics traditionally distributed through newspapers and libraries. There are variations in both components and names (teletext, viewdata, Prestel, Telidon), but services are similar. Subscribers can limit their attention to the types of material of interest to them. In a fraction of the time previously required to search through volumes of data, lawyers and doctors can prepare to deal with individual cases. The British, French, and Germans have moved faster than Americans in installing this system, but United States newspapers have begun experimental ventures. Costs of the operation limit its initial adoption to the largest markets.

Cable's interactive capacity can extend the classroom into the home and create new opportunities for continuing education. By cable or satellite, health care can be provided to remote areas. From a centralized location specialists can submit diagnoses and advice to scattered clinics. Irvine, California, has connected 24 of its schools, its colleges, science center, city hall, and school district office by two-way cable. Graduate students in education can watch teachers in action and ask questions by TV when the class is over. Fourth-grade students from one school can share their drawings and book reports with students and teachers in other schools. One instructor can teach English to non-English-speaking young people in schools all over Irvine. Travel and time can be saved in holding teachers' meetings; refresher courses can be made easily available for school personnel.

In Reading, Pennsylvania, the Berks Cable Company furnishes an interactive system making it possible for programming to originate from 64 locations. A weekly program, "Inside City Hall," allows citizens to talk by cable with their mayor and city council members. From any of the originating centers this can be done through split screens and monitors on a face-to-face basis. From homes, viewers can respond by telephone. Similar procedures allow citizens to participate in city budget meetings and other governmental deliberations. On certain occasions community tensions have been resolved by this method. Reading's mayor has said that the city has come to depend on such exchanges and could never "go back to the old way, being satisfied with one person's showing up for a public hearing."

The spread of home computers increases the interactive capability of the other electronic media. A computer now selling for $1000 is said to have the capacity of an early model costing one million dollars. The instruments help farmers to conduct their agribusiness in a well-informed and carefully planned manner.

Time magazine replaced its annual "Man of the Year" in January 1983 with the personal computer as the "Machine of the Year." In Chapter 4 we will deal with implications of this development, especially in education.

Religious broadcasting

From the beginning of radio broadcasting there have been Christians who have been optimistic about electronic possibilities for the church. Most initiative has been demonstrated either by independent, evangelical agencies or by visionary individuals belonging to mainline denominations but operating outside the bureaucratic framework.

The first religious broadcast in 1921 was a vespers service over KDKA from Calvary Episcopal Church in Pittsburg, Pennsylvania, certainly a mainline congregation. There is an interesting historical footnote, however: the senior pastor saw so little significance in the occasion that he delegated the task of conducting the service to a junior associate.

By contrast, Paul Rader of the Chicago Gospel Tabernacle plunged into extensive use of radio in 1922. He arranged to use the idle studios of WBBM for 14 hours each Sunday. Soon the regular worship services at the Tabernacle were crowded with people attracted by the broadcasts. Later he launched a network program, "Breakfast Brigade," on CBS.

Meanwhile Walter A. Maier, of the Lutheran Church Missouri Synod, had begun preaching on local sustaining (unpaid) time, and in 1930 took the ambitious step of contracting with the Columbia Broadcasting System for $200,000 to broadcast weekly for a year. No denominational funds were involved. Youth and lay people pledged $100,000, and the rest was to be raised from the audience. This was the beginning of "The Lutheran Hour" and its supporting body, the Lutheran Laymen's League. Later the program was carried on the Mutual network and now is syndicated. With Maier, and later (until recently) Oswald Hoffman, as speakers, "The Lutheran Hour" has attracted a loyal audience, many of whom are members of other denominations.

Other pioneers included H.M.S. Richards with "The Voice of

Prophecy" and Charles E. Fuller, whose "Old-Fashioned Revival Hour" continued beyond his retirement in 1967 and is now called "The Joyful Sound."

Ecumenical Protestantism was not oblivious to electronic opportunities. As stations and networks were confronted with multiple requests from religious groups for airtime, they turned to cooperative agencies to arrange for appropriate representation. The Federal Council and later the National Council of Churches aired "The National Radio Pulpit," with S. Parkes Cadman and a succession of speakers including Harry Emerson Fosdick, Ralph Sockman, and David H. C. Read. Norman Vincent Peale became prominent on "The Art of Living." Among Roman Catholic programs were "The Ava Maria Hour" and "The Catholic Hour," and Jews were represented by a dramatic series, "The Eternal Light," featuring some of the best scripts ever written for radio. Denominations and independent groups who chose not to be affiliated with ecumenical councils did not participate in the allocation of free time and many began to purchase time.

Changes with television

As television became pervasive, the prewar pattern of religious broadcasting was gradually altered. Both national and local councils of churches had always opposed the use of paid time by members, maintaining that stations licensed to operate "in the public interest, convenience, and necessity" were obligated to grant free time for something so socially significant as religion. Television, however, was a much more expensive medium to operate than radio, and station owners were reluctant to grant time to anyone without payment. Gradually, too, the financial circumstances of both radio and television stations changed until there was so much demand for commercial time that sustaining openings were nearly eliminated from many schedules. Meanwhile federal regulation became weaker and weaker until stations felt no pressure to provide public service time. Evangelical independents had founded their own agency, National Religious Broadcasters, partly to counteract opposition to commercial religious radio. While mainline denominations were talking about evangelism and staffing evangelism departments, independent groups were willing to invest substantial sums in something they regarded as a powerful medium of outreach. The independents have grown; mainline churches have lost members. While broadcasting may not have caused the difference, its use reveals a significant attitude: a fervent desire to share the gospel and a willingness to wrestle with the mind-set of the uncommitted.

A few mainline denominations eventually became convinced that limiting their efforts to sustaining time was becoming self-defeating, and in 1978 the Communication Commission of the National Council altered its policy and removed the all-out opposition to purchase of time by churches.

The national cooperative agencies continued their somewhat feeble use of the networks' token grants of time by producing "Directions" on ABC, "Frontiers of Faith," and then specials, on NBC, and "For Our Time" on CBS. CBS originally had two one-half hour programs, "Look Up and Live" and "Lamp Unto My Feet," but they were replaced by one-half hour of "For Our Time," with the understanding that religion would be featured regularly on the news program "Sunday Morning." Within a short time viewers of that series searched in vain for religious elements.

In defense of the networks it must be admitted that few of their member stations choose to carry the religious series offered them, and churches have done little to build audiences for the programs. Some denominations have placed emphasis on their own series: for example, the Lutheran Church Missouri Synod with "This is the Life," the Lutheran Church in America with "Davey and Goliath," Methodists and the American Lutheran Church with mini-series, and the Seventh Day Adventists with "Faith for To-day." Among Catholics the Paulists have distributed the weekly program "Insight." Various denominations distribute spot announcements because they can often be placed without payment on stations, but their effectiveness is questionable. Locally many congregations broadcast services on sustaining or commercial time, and there is often concrete evidence of listener-viewer appreciation, despite negative advice from national media experts.

Electronic church

Rising above this pusillanimous plateau has emerged what is called the electronic church, dominated by the personalities of Pat Robertson, Jim Bakker, Rex Humbard, Oral Roberts, Jerry Falwell, Robert Schuller, James Kennedy, Jimmy Swaggart, and Billy Graham. There are great differences within this list. Some are establishing their own ecclesiastical empires; others attempt to relate closely to existing congregations. Some offer religious versions of variety shows; others stay with more traditional presentations. But among them they invest hundreds of millions of dollars a year and their income is dependent on the application of computerized fund-raising to television. At least two series, "The 700 Club" and "PTL," are on the air or cable once or more daily in many markets.

The discovery that religious broadcasting can be big business has affected even the ownership of stations, especially radio. In 1928 there were approximately 60 stations related to religious agencies, but with the technical restrictions imposed by the old Federal Radio Commission this number was reduced to 33 in 1930. Of those, 12 remain, including WCAL, St. Olaf College (founded in 1922), KFUO, St. Louis, Missouri (1925), and WMBI, Moody Bible Institute station (1926). Between 1945 and 1960 approximately 10 stations per year turned to religion for a substantial part or all of their programming, and by the 80s there are more than 1000 such stations, with many operating commercially. Twenty-five TV stations have a religious orientation and the number will increase with the introduction of low-power television.

Roman Catholics have established a Telecommunications Network not only to distribute TV programs but also to provide data-processing, electronic mail, telephone and teleconferencing services. Three hours of radio and television programs are offered every day, five days a week. Some 89 of 172 U.S. dioceses expressed interest in participating during the network's first three years. The network began operating in September 1982 and within a few months had 37 affiliated dioceses. One estimate of the start-up costs was five million dollars.

Mother Angelica distributes "The Eternal Word" by satellite and attempts to operate without on-the-air appeals. The Mormons have a nationwide satellite network and other denominations are experimenting with this means of transmission. Many congregations are beginning to use computers, and video cassettes are increasingly common.

With all of this ferment in the current response of churches to the coming of the electronic age, many questions bubble to the surface. Who actually pays attention to electronically distributed religious material? Is there any genuine outreach? Do the programs strengthen or weaken the church? Are all of these media valid instruments for communication of the faith, or do we suffer from contamination by association? Why have mainline churches been so hesitant in comparison with so-called evangelicals? What should we be doing to take advantage of valid opportunities? We will return to such questions in Part 2 of this book, after we have balanced the pros and cons associated with the influence of the new media on society in general.

What to Expect 3
from Broadcasting

Potentially, radio and television are marvelous instruments for informing and entertaining. They may also distort values, sensationalize news, inhibit learning, and contribute to antisocial behavior. Which is more likely to prevail, the Jekyll or Hyde characteristics?

Reflection of problems

The media reflect many problems they do not cause. Columnist Erma Bombeck contrasted media violence with actual happenings in Guatemala, Beirut, Afghanistan, and South Africa. She claimed that children could distinguish between fantasy and reality and said it was reality that bothered her.

In another column Sydney Harris cited a study indicating that most children would rather do things with their parents than watch television, and he commented: "But if parents don't want to bother, then TV 'violence' is an easy copout for their own dereliction of duty."

Sociologist Daniel Bell finds at least one root of materialism outside the media. He regards the installment plan, or instant credit, as "the greatest engine in the destruction of the Protestant ethic," and claims this in turn popularized the demand for instant gratification.

The influence of broadcasting is often exaggerated because of the millions of dollars invested in it by advertisers. Selling products people already want is one thing; changing basic attitudes and convictions is another. The media, by themselves, are unlikely to reverse deeply held convictions. Instead, they serve primarily to reinforce existing attitudes and to trigger superficial impulses. One study revealed that citizens who watched the most broadcasts in political campaigns were least likely to change their voting.

When critics trace contemporary marital standards to the near-absence of "normal" marriages on television today, they overlook the fact that a generation ago only "normal" marriages were allowed on camera, but this did not prevent radical changes in connubial customs. NBC's Brandon Tartikoff has said that the guidelines for network standards "drift three or four degrees to the left each year, just like society does."

The allegedly pernicious influence of electronic news is modified by surveys showing that nearly two-thirds of U.S. adults read at least part of some newspaper every day and nearly one-third read *Time*, *Newsweek*, or *U.S. News and World Report* weekly.

The common complaint that popular media contain an excess of bad news must be balanced against the importance of openness in a democratic society. Even in tension-filled situations, recognizing disagreements and hazards is a necessary step toward reconciliation. There is no progress toward better relationships between blacks and whites, for example, without an honest airing of grievances. Almost the only media to exclude bad news are found in totalitarian societies.

Speculation

Even if they do not cause many of society's problems, the media may affect them in important ways. Nearly everyone has an opinion about the nature of that effect, good or bad. We are all experts because we are all listeners and viewers.

Media philosophers seem to be infected by the virus of sensationalism and they contribute little to a substantial understanding of what's happening.

Marshall McLuhan claimed that print was extinct and wrote more than a dozen books to prove it. One academic critic summarized his work: "Although McLuhan's ideas are often intuitively appealing, they rarely lend themselves to logical analysis or scientific verification." In nontechnical language he is saying that the pundit's claims do not make good sense. McLuhan's distinction between hot and cold media and the descriptions of different media as extensions of human beings simply do not hold up under thoughtful analysis. McLuhan could be thoroughly consistent in rejecting rational thought as an element in communication because he so carefully avoided it in his own writing.

William Stephenson and Tony Schwartz are also faddists. Stephenson's *Play Theory of Mass Communication* narrowly selects only material to support his view that everything conveyed through the media is transferred into diversionary entertainment. He disregards an abundance of contradictory evidence. Tony Schwartz regards human beings as an early stage in the evolution of computers and tells how to push the right buttons to get desired responses. As partial observations the writings of McLuhan, Stephenson, and Schwartz are stimulating; as comprehensive descriptions they are misleading.

Fortunately there are modern students of communication who dig beneath the superficial speculation of pioneers. Recent research is not based on the belief that ideas are transmitted by hypodermic-like injections. Neither content alone nor the exotic form of symbols is assumed to be the only determining factor in the process. Human relationships are seen as central in any evaluative study of communication.

Research findings

In published reports of recent research it is obvious that modern psychology has shifted attention from stimulus-response models to a view of individuals as playing an active and selective, and not simply a reactive, role. People are recognized as more than puppets and the media as less than automatically influential. For significant findings, it is recognized that observation must be made in the situations where listening and viewing actually occur, not under contrived laboratory conditions. Backgrounds, predispositions, needs, and expectations must be taken into account in attempting to measure results. Consideration must be given to the subtle, cumulative effects of the media.

Some of the findings of such research are obvious, others are inconclusive. At least there is a minimum of exaggerated claims.

It comes as no surprise to "learn" from one study that "children not coerced into watching favor humorous over nonhumorous television." Another less than astounding report concludes that "presentations whose form neither bores nor overloads the viewer will lead to higher levels of learning."

Studies of sex and violence avoid futile preoccupation with numbers of incidents and pursue the nature of exploitative sex and gratuitous violence. Apart from the obvious fact that some unstable persons are triggered by media exposure into such ventures as high-jacking and poisoning with nonprescription drugs, the influence of the media on most persons is still the subject of considerable doubt.

Prolonged exposure to media violence seems to cause some people to regard violence as an acceptable way to resolve conflicts; blue-uniformed "good guys" make violence respectable. Others, however, may become more active in opposition to violence and still others may become almost immune, inclined passively to observe violence in others. Presentation of gory, realistic war scenes may inflame militarists or promote pacifism. Heavy exposure to urban violence sometimes creates unreasonable fears but also stimulates a demand for hardnosed response.

Like the tobacco industry challenging reports from the Surgeon General's office, the broadcasting industry can produce research concluding that "television is not causally implicated in the development of behavior among children and adolescents." Less prejudiced scholars have concluded, however, that there are still many unanswered questions concerning the actual effects of the mass media in such areas as sex, violence, and inhibition of the learning process. In much research of the past, audiences have been regarded as unthinking reactors to electronic stimuli. Instead, humans are complex creatures who may respond in totally different ways from the intentions and expectations of program producers. We may absorb, reject, or reprocess material, depending on a host of personal factors.

The inconclusiveness of present research is no reason for tranquility. George Gerbner and his communication research associates have written: "The observable independent contributions of television can only be relatively small. But just as an average temperature shift of a few degrees can lead to an ice age, or the outcome of elections can be determined by slight margins, so too can a relatively small but pervasive influence make a crucial difference. The 'size' of an 'effect' is far less critical than the direction of its steady contribution."

People can do little about the approach of an ice age, but we may influence the direction taken by the electronic age. There is no doubt that the media can have long-range, negative effects. There is also evidence that this result is not inevitable.

Public taste

Hopes for constructive use of the media are dimmed by evidence of public taste. Audience surveys generally support the description of television by one humorist as "chewing gum for the eyeballs."

Surveys of what people *would like* to see on television often produce quite different projections from what they actually watch. "Who Shot J.R.?" on the "Dallas" series attracted a larger audience than any program previously aired. The formula for this series combines a luxurious life style, raw sex, conniving, and corruption. Howard Rosenbery of the *Los Angeles Times* wrote, " 'Dallas' lifted trash to exquisite and exhilarating heights that few series have been able to match." Its appeal has not been limited to Americans. In West Germany 45% of the TV households have tuned to it. In Bangladesh it was second in national ratings only to a locally produced drama. In South Africa, J.R. and company have recorded the highest ratings ever.

Such a portrayal of American life contributes little to international understanding and in some countries it is banned for its cultural imperialism, but its global reception supports the biblical view of human nature.

"Dallas" is not unique in its reflection of public taste. Of the top 50 shows in U.S. network television's first 20 years, eight are episodes from the "Beverly Hillbillies." In New York City 10,000 to 15,000 callers a day pay to listen by telephone to a one-minute soap opera. Game shows obviously appeal to envy and covetousness.

The industry can be accused of exploiting such inclinations, but education and religion can also be indicted for failing to contribute to the development of a more enlightened public.

The bottom line

American broadcasting does pander to the lowest of tastes and instincts because of its commercial orientation. We are the only nation in the world where merchandizing has become the primary function of the media. This was not true in the beginning. With the first broadcasts Herbert Hoover, then Secretary of Commerce, said: "It is inconceivable that we should allow so great a possibility for service, for news, for education, and for vital commercial purposes, to be drowned in advertising chatter." He predicted that the American people would never stand for advertising on the radio.

The financial structure of American broadcasting has made it an audience-delivery business. Series are planned, produced, and changed in whatever ways are necessary to attract listeners and viewers to give attention to the commercials. Programs are bait to hook buyers. It is essential that "demographics" include the highest percentage of likely purchasers of the product being advertised, most often women ages 18 to 49. The bottom line is in sales, not service to society.

Even news, once regarded as a financially unproductive operation performed to retain a license, has become so popular and therefore so commercially valuable, that standards are threatened. As Andy Rooney of CBS has warned, "As soon as we pay more attention to what people want to hear than what they ought to know, we're sales persons."

Most Americans are not too unhappy with this situation. How else could people get such "free" entertainment? Critics contend that broadcasting is not really free; users invest heavily in equipment, and program costs are allegedly passed along as increased prices of advertised products. The cost of tickets to theaters and sporting events, however, makes the price of television sets a good investment. And advertisers can claim that commercials make possible mass production and distribution, thus lowering consumer prices. A Roper survey has even indicated that nearly three-fourths of Americans find commercials fun to watch. This could be because many more dollars-per-minute are invested in them than in programs.

Meanwhile, with little public clamor, a potential instrument of enlightenment is being used almost exclusively for a different purpose. Given free reign, leaders of the industry are generally unconcerned about the social influences of the media they dominate. This is understandable; they are in business to make profits, a function not inevitably contributing to the public welfare. Even Adam Smith, patron saint of free enterprise, admitted that merchants' concerns for their own investments might blind them to public interests. He said, "The government of an exclusive company of merchants is, perhaps, the worst of all governments for any country whatsoever."

Some broadcasters complain that they are subject to criticism not directed to the stage or films, where artists may be celebrated for entertaining without any pretense of enlightenment or positive social influence. But broadcasting is inherently different from the stage and cinema, which use no public resource comparable to the airwaves, consume limited amounts of time, and do not penetrate homes. Radio and TV are so pervasive that their operation raises distinctive public issues.

Corporate responsibility

Some sponsors and broadcasters realize this. A memo stating Xerox policy in planning one series read: "Each program will have an over-purpose—it will not only entertain, it will tend to stretch the mind, to inspire, to stir the conscience, and require thought. Our programs should try to advance television over what it has been. Where possible we should use our money to lead, not follow."

The president of Quaker Oats Company, acknowledging complaints about children's television, wrote: "U.S. broadcasters have operating control of one of the most economically and socially important assets—the U.S. broadcast spectrum—in the world today. . . . We at Quaker Oats believe that the key to corporate responsibility is for the business community to encourage, not evade, discussion of those problems that arise when the activities of business conflict with the needs and concerns of society. We think this is particularly true in the case of children's television. We only wish we could get others in the broadcast and television industry to agree with us."

William S. Paley, reflecting on his long career as head of the Columbia Broadcasting System, has recalled: "I began to pay attention to finding worthwhile and cultural programs to balance the music and variety shows in order to help improve the reputation of CBS for good taste and social responsibility." He advocated a kind of balance—giving most of the people what they want most of the time, but including in the schedule at least a few programs of higher quality. Realizing that this would handicap his network in the rush for ratings, he devised a plan to divide the loss and, hopefully, develop an audience for better programs. He proposed that six hours of high quality programming be made available every week, two hours for each network. The plan was rejected and Paley's disappointment with deteriorating standards, due to the "paralyzing effect of network competition on high quality programming," is evident in his book *As It Happened*.

Where the buck stops

One excuse often advanced for shoddy programming on radio and TV is the enormous volume of production required. This does preclude the regular appearance of masterpieces, but creative artists, including producers, claim they could present a much better product if they were less restricted by commercial domination. Not long ago the Caucus for Producers, Writers and Directors, including some of the top names in television, issued a statement admitting that most of prime-time TV is drab and blaming the network bureaucracy. Specifically, they listed these reasons for the slide into mediocrity:

- Network overreliance on testing and ratings leads to a bland, repetitive diet for viewers.
- The demand that every program be no. 1 in its time slot, instead of a respectable no. 2 or no. 3, concentrates on appealing to the lowest common denominator.
- The intensity of network competition results in schedules being announced later each year, and changed impetuously, preventing producers from having enough time to do their job.
- Network executives constantly interfere in the creative process, with harmful results.

Grant Tinker, a vocal member of the caucus, later became NBC chairman and defended his network's schedule by explaining, "I've come down off that quality kick I used to be on."

Critics claim that, in the present network atmosphere, programs like "All in the Family" and "60 Minutes," which began with low ratings, would not be given time to survive. "Hill Street Blues" and its medical version, "St. Elsewhere," challenge this view. They were kept on the air, despite low ratings, in hopes of gradually attracting numbers of viewers who prefer realism to escapism.

Such patience, however, is unusual because it is easier to peddle drugs. Producer Aaron Spelling of "Charlie's Angels," "Mod Squad," and "Fantasy Island," has been quoted as saying, "I am giving people a happy pill." Paul Klein, once in charge of programs at NBC, summarized his policies: "Thought is a tune-out. So is education. Melodrama is good. A little tear here and there, a little morality tale. That's good. . . . One of the qualities I look for is fake realism, the illusion you're getting something meaningful. Then you overlay that with what I call trash. . . . It's the ideal content to fit the nature of 'waste time,' which is what people use the media for." Since Klein did not produce high ratings he was soon replaced, but his approach outlasted his tenure.

Jerry Mander once tried to use TV to promote ecology and said the attempt was "like throwing snowballs at a tank."

Once in awhile someone demonstrates what is possible in broadcasting. One episode of "Roots" attracted a higher rating than any previous regularly scheduled program, and seven other programs in the series were viewed by more than 40% of the available audience. Promotion is important; Mobil invested heavily in publicizing one syndication of "Nicholas Nickelby," and in San Francisco it achieved a 26% rating. Phil Donahue has proven that even a daytime audience can be interested in serious issues, often alternating with sensational and titillating topics.

The most influential people in broadcasting, commercial network executives, are more likely to take the easy route of peddling happy pills than the more difficult road of enlightening audiences without boring them. Ted Turner, hyperactive entrepreneur, told the Veterans of Foreign Wars, "The people running the three networks are the greatest enemies the United States has ever had. . . . They're tearing the country down from the inside. . . . Their only standard for programming is how much money they can make on something and they shirk all sorts of responsibility for what they carry. And they're all real sad about it, too. Every one of them will tell you privately—they've all told me privately— to the effect that they're very ashamed of what they do."

Christians are familiar with the human condition in which "the good that I would, I do not." We know that in society there must be some restrictions on the pursuit of self-interest. Democracy provides for checks and balances, but these are being removed from American broadcasting by deregulation. The Federal Communications Commission, charged with representing the public, is abandoning its responsibilities and removing all meaningful standards previously governing operation of the public media. If present conditions continue we can only expect from commercial broadcasting more commercialism, more frivolous entertainment, and even less concern for public affairs and constructive social influence. In a later chapter we will consider possible citizen response to this erosion.

Religious broadcasting

What about the expansion of religious broadcasting? Won't this help to counteract the influences of the secular media? Available evidence indicates that the attraction of the so-called electronic church has been exaggerated. Rex Humbard's publicity materials once claimed more than 100 million viewers, while he now admits that the weekly figure is probably less than 2 million. Jerry Falwell was claiming 25 million viewers when he had approximately 1.4 million. The combined audience of more than 60 syndicated religious television programs was estimated at 22 million in the late 1970s, but a more recent survey puts the number of regular viewers to church-sponsored programs at 13.3 million. Because of the variation in methods of calculation, all of these figures have only limited significance.

We know that most viewers of religious telecasts are already church-related, modifying claims for outreach of the media. It is also true, however, that the total of unchurched viewers is larger than the number of unchurched attending regular worship services.

No more than half a dozen religious telecasts attract more than a million viewers weekly, and all of them are presented by independent broadcasters unconnected with historic denominations. Mainline churches have never made much of a dent in national use of the media, and their influence is not likely to increase. Lack of unity handicaps the church in its negotiations and in its impact.

The National Council of Churches continues to cooperate with networks in producing a few programs, but since they are not sponsored commercially, fewer and fewer stations carry them and audience size is limited. Weekly series have been replaced by occasional "specials." Remaining locally originated religious programs are being moved to earlier Sunday morning times. It is ironic that at a time when American stations are reducing the minutes devoted to religion, broadcasting companies in the socialist countries of eastern Europe are beginning to allow churches to go on the air.

There is also little inclination on the part of most denominational executives to take seriously either the threat from or the potential of the modern media. There may be a link between that abdication and the decline of religious influence on government, education, and society in general. Eric Sevareid has warned that the danger of broadcasting becoming no more than show business is due partly to the fact that "traditional messages from the intellectual community and churches became weak and confused in this long period of aimlessness."

Locally, some congregations do contradict advice from national experts and broadcast their services, but they seldom give attention to the technical quality of the pickup or, more importantly, engage in follow-up with listener-viewers.

Whether or not religious broadcasts, presented primarily by independent evangelists, strengthen or detract from the work of the Christian church is a hotly debated question which will be examined in Part 2. For now we will only say that we cannot expect religious broadcasting, as presently conducted, to wield much influence on American society.

What to Expect 4
from the Newer Media

Just because new gadgets are invented does not mean that people will use them. In 1890 there were Britons excited by the prospect of bringing the sounds of London theater into the home by telephone, but Victorian Electrophone proved to be no more than a historical curiosity. Ma Bell's picture phone has not become a household instrument in 25 years. Forty years ago there were predictions that facsimile would soon replace newspapers.

Exaggerated fears and hopes

Both fears and hopes aroused by new media can be exaggerated. In Oliver Cromwell's day the new postal service was feared because of speculation that letters would be opened by the ill-intentioned. President A. Bartlett Giamatti of Yale has warned that today "the computer has been invested with magical power; if you were to believe our aroused press, the computer is the intellectual equivalent of the anabolic steroid, destined to turn six-year olds into Olympians of competency testing." He claims, "The only predictable results of this silliness will be, in a few years, strong reaction against the exaggerated claims for computing and word processing. So it will go until the media marching band passes on to the next issue."

One columnist has speculated about what would have happened if electronics had been developed before printing. Then newspapers would be a new phenomenon and the possibilities would be exciting. Instead of watching little green letters on an illuminated screen, a person could have an entire news and entertainment package delivered at the door each day. A person could leaf through sections, cut out interesting articles, carry the paper to remote areas or on the train. Finally, it could be used to start fires or line garbage pails.

In anticipating developments from new media, allowance must be made for both the exuberance of media enthusiasts and the natural resistance of many humans to any form of change. Failure to recognize the inevitability of some changes, however, is the surest way to doom institutions and societies. Whether we believe it or not, whether we like it or not, new media such as cable, satellites, and especially computers, are already beginning to make changes demanding our attention. In 1984 several cable networks moved into profitability, demonstrating that this medium can indeed survive.

Within a few years many homes will be equipped with information centers allowing residents to view the latest news without delivery of a newspaper; to receive and send messages by electronic mail; to perform occupational tasks without leaving home, transmitting memos across miles within seconds; to confer with different colleagues concerning changes in a document all can examine on their screens; to bank and shop without battling traffic; to make recreational choices from a host of options; and to monitor deliberations of the city council, registering opinions on crucial issues. As we adopt such revisions in our ways of communicating, certain questions must be addressed.

Will the new media give us access to greater diversity or merely more of the same kind of information and entertainment? Are human beings likely to take advantage of technical opportunities for interaction and participation, or will most people simply find new channels for diversion? Can anything be done about the cluster of accompanying social dangers—threatened unemployment, violation of privacy, raiding information banks? What are implications from the new media for the church? These are the directions to be explored in this chapter.

Genuine diversity?

Cable, satellites, and the recently authorized increase in over-the-air stations will undoubtedly result in more program services. Whether there will be any greater variety among the offerings is another question.

In theory there will now be so many programming agencies trying to attract listeners and viewers that some will have to settle for smaller audiences by catering to specialized interests and tastes. This has already happened with radio in some large cities. In Houston, Texas, one station scheduled only Beatles music, playing only records featuring John, Paul, George, and Ringo. One proposal for low-power TV would cover only New York's Chinatown. Independent superstations such as WTBS in Atlanta can give networks competition by offering—through satellite and cable—sports, movies, and even news. Some observers have predicted that the three-network share of the television audience, once more than 90%, will drop to 60% by 1990, but an initial decline in that figure seems to be leveling off.

Even the prospect of added competition is no guarantee of an increase in socially constructive programs, reflecting accepted ideals, traditions, and values. Some of the sales appeal of cable has been based on the regular availability of films featuring explicit sex. Even in the daytime there is a rash of programs, under the guise of counseling, prodding participants into revealing the most intimate of sexual problems.

At least two national cable services featuring more substantive programming have already failed to survive. CBS cable, created to corner an audience segment inclined to arts and culture, collapsed after being in business less than a year and losing at least 30 million dollars. The Entertainment Channel, a joint Rockefeller Center-RCA enterprise featuring quality inputs from Britain, was disbanded after nine months.

The main hope for new broadcasting services to society is focused in the public access provisions of cable. So many channels are available to cable operators that, from the beginning, there has been pressure on the companies granted franchises to set aside a proportion of these outlets for use by community groups.

Under 1972 FCC Rules, operators were required to provide studio facilities and channel capacity to allow citizens to produce original, local programming.

Use of these channels has been spotty, resulting in both the worst and the best programs imaginable. In some communities schools, churches, and community groups have taken advantage of the opportunity for immediate, live contact with their constituencies. In many localities there are forums on public affairs.

Producing even the simplest program for TV requires a measure of competence and an investment of time. Frequently a few enthusiasts undertake a local production schedule beyond their capacity to continue, and there is disillusionment on the part of both station operators and community groups. At the same time there is an increasing threat to those access channels from commercial pressures. In 1979 the FCC virtually deregulated cable, and Congress is more likely to be responsive to the preferences of a big, publicly influential business than to the cautions of an unorganized scattering of citizens concerned for the public welfare.

This is not a new predicament. It is almost a repeat of a situation which occurred in 1934. During congressional debate on the Communications Act, a proposed Wagner/Hatfield amendment recommended that 25% of the radio spectrum be set aside for use by educational, religious, agricultural, cooperative, and similar nonprofit-making associations. Commercial stations were successful in defeating the amendment, partly by assuring legislators that there was no need for such an action; the industry would certainly provide sufficient time for the public interests included in the amendment. Similar assurances by cable operators today are discounted by educators and religious leaders, whose access to the public media has eroded to the point of insignificance.

Unless the public wakes up to the importance of public access, the extension of cable will have little positive effect on television. There will be even more diversionary entertainment but no more communication of democratic and religious values. Complainers about TV will have forfeited one chance to remedy the situation.

Public broadcasting

One agency devoted to more than merchandising is public broadcasting. It is not a new medium, because it has been operating on a limited basis since the beginning of radio, but it is only in recent years, partly because of satellite interconnection, that it has emerged as a "fourth network." It is becoming recognized as the principal source of media diversity, the main alternative to commercial radio and TV. More than 68% of all American households watch public television for some part of the week.

In 1978 the Carnegie Commission on the Future of Public Broadcasting came to significant conclusions, most of which are being overlooked. The commission recognized that the United States is the only western nation relying so exclusively upon advertising effectiveness as the standard for its broadcasting activities and stated:

> The idea of broadcasting as a force in the public interest, a display case for the best of America's creative arts, a forum for public debate—advancing the democratic conversation and enhancing the public imagination—has receded before the inexorable force of audience maximization.

The commission looked ahead:

> The power of the communications media must be marshaled in the interest of human development, not merely for advertising revenue. . . . As television and radio are joined by a host of new technological advances, the need becomes even more urgent for a nonprofit institution that can assist the nation in reducing the lag between the introduction of new telecommunications devices and their widespread social benefit.

Advocating the development of a public telecommunications complex serving the entire country, the commission acknowledged that if radio and television had evolved in this country with a "fuller definition of public service," the need for an alternative institution would be less critical. Under existing conditions, however, the commission concluded it could turn only to a public instrument to "bring Americans together, teach us, and inspire us."

Attempts to build a structure incorporating this vision are handicapped by financial limitations and public apathy. Government funding has been reduced, but this source is suspect anyway because an agency dependent on government grants is always subject to fiscal starvation out of fear or revenge. A truly independent medium of communication is bound, at times, to confront the establishment in what appears to be an adversarial relationship. Somehow the funding for PBS must not be dependent on the whims of administrators or legislators. Turning to corporations for support opens the agency to the same commercial influence as its competitors. The only proposal avoiding both dangers would secure a percentage of the enormous revenues of commercial stations to be allocated to PBS. Opposition from industry, of course, is predictably vigorous. Meanwhile, investment in homes for cable and pay TV may cut into contributions for public stations.

Under present limitations, PBS proceeds courageously in its attempt to provide an attractive alternative to commercial programming. Whether its support, financially and otherwise, grows or declines will depend partly on the degree of audience disenchantment with the competition.

Grass-roots democracy

While radio and TV can be accused of encouraging passive listening and viewing, the newer media of two-way cable and especially computers stimulate interaction, participation, and involvement. There are new prospects for the real exchange which constitutes communication and results in learning.

A two-way cable system may offer only an elementary form of interaction. When, for example, a talk show host only invites viewers to register their agreement or disagreement with a guest, there is no opportunity for dialog. Even such simple responses may, however, help persons to be more alert and discriminating in their viewing. One interactive device allows viewers to select optional segments of the same program. For example, the order of items on a newscast can be rearranged, and expanded coverage of certain stories can be chosen. This system is already workable technically, with taped programs, but is questionable financially.

Some analysts are so euphoric about the interactive capabilities of computers connected with cable or satellites that they suggest that the very shape of our representative democracy may be altered. The philosopher Jacques Ellul wrote, "When dialogue begins, propaganda ends." One letter to *Time* about its Machine of the Year issue proposes: "They should be installed in every home. We could then be plugged into Washington and vote on all issues, thus eliminating Congress." It is difficult to imagine such a national process as more than a pooling of ignorance, but in dealing with community issues it may have some value.

Local officials can hold town meetings with citizens in their homes. Issues can be explored in depth and at length, with full opportunity for questioning and discussion.

How will this affect politicians? There is a popular belief that television exposes phonies, but I believe this to be true only of amateur phonies. Professional actors have learned to convey character in so convincing a manner that they are able to project an apparent sincerity regardless of their actual convictions. Not only can actors become politicians; politicians can learn acting.

Viewers aware of potential deceit will be able, through the new media, to express their disbelief and possibly alter the direction taken by Madison Avenue. Publicized weaknesses in American autos have forced manufacturers to improve production standards and notify the public concerning changes. Except for its news coverage, television does not enjoy great public confidence. With the increase in opportunities to react to programs and ads, citizens may be able to demonstrate that we are less gullible than believed. This depends, of course, on improved consumer education.

If two-way cable ever becomes fully operational, with its actual opportunity for exchange of ideas, interaction will be changed from theory into reality. Then we will discover how much democracy is really desired.

Computers in education

The main hope from electronics for increased interaction lies with computers. This sounds strange in light of accusations that video arcades allow children to become obsessed with a machine and keep them from associating with others. Recent studies indicate that video games are more of a passing fad than a threat, but even the arcades have their defenders. Juvenile crime expert B. David Brooks has claimed that they represent "social places like the old corner ice cream parlor . . . that help loners come out of their shells." He said that unpopular youngsters, such as those who are overweight, handicapped, or shy, attain respect from other kids by developing skill at games. Active participation in video games cannot be seen as much of an advancement beyond passive TV watching, but other uses of computers are more important.

In school, too, the computer may stimulate rather than retard social contact. A University of Minnesota researcher, studying the reaction of preschool children, concluded, "The computer was challenging and new enough for the kids to like to work on it together." At least 80% of the time the youngsters worked in pairs at the computer, she reported, while in another corner of the playroom children worked alone about 80% of the time in putting together jigsaw puzzles.

Such socializing may be due to the novelty of the devices, but more important than contact with others in the same room is the connection with other minds and sources of information throughout the world. Adults with a built-in resistance to anything new, and especially anything mechanical, can advance all sorts of arguments against the widespread use of computers. I do not need a computer to balance my checkbook. I can pay bills by telephone without a computer. I *like* browsing through the library.

Meanwhile children and young people are discovering that some aspects of learning can be as much fun as playing a game. No college hoping to attract top students can be without computer facilities. In some fields of graduate study students are now required to have terminals at home, connected to the university's computer.

Enthusiasts expect computers to become as ubiquitous in our society as the automobile and television. One study has estimated that there will be 80 million personal computers in use in the United States within 10-15 years.

If only partly true, this glimpse of the future has major implications for education. The microcomputer has been described in *American Education*, a magazine published by the U.S. Department of Education, as "potentially the most revolutionary educational innovation since the printing press."

Psychologist B. F. Skinner told a session of the American Psychological Convention that computers are a cure for the ailing U.S. educational system. He cited the video game fad as an example of how reinforcement of positive behavior, like rewarding a good game with a high score, can hold a student's interest and enhance learning.

Research, especially in recent studies, indicates that students do better on examinations when they have computer-assisted instruction. Introduction of computers in school systems is increasing steadily. 1983 estimates indicated one computer for every 200 American public school students; within 10 years the ratio is expected to shrink to "something more like one computer to every four students," according to Prof. David Moursund of the University of Oregon, president of the International Council for Computers in Education.

Computers have special value for children with hearing impairments or other learning disabilities. There is even special equipment such as an eyebrow switch and a voice synthesizer that can make computers accessible to paralyzed students.

One fallout from the spread of computers may be a stretching of the differences among primary and secondary schools. Poorer school districts may lack the resources to equip classrooms with computers, handicapping their graduates.

Families will be under increasing pressure to purchase computers for children. One manufacturer began the exploitation with TV spots portraying parents waving happy good-byes to a son leaving for college, then sadly meeting the train on his return in disappointment, an obvious failure because he had been deprived of a computer. Making the point unmistakable, a voice suggested, "Instead of saving for an education, maybe you should spend a little now!"

Will home computers place a greater strain on American families? Or will they enlighten young and old, bringing them together in the adventure of learning? A research project at New York University is investigating these questions. At an estimated cost of $750,000, the study will examine the effects of the computer on the quality of learning as well as on the quality of family life. Research will begin with the assumption that a child's interaction with the machine makes the experience fundamentally different from watching television.

If experience with television is any indication, there will be many studies with inconclusive and contradictory findings. One result is safely predictable: some people will make significant, constructive use of computers, others will not. "Successful" users will recognize the limitations of the instruments, as noted by Massachusetts Institute of Technology computer professor Joseph Weizenbaum: "The assertion that all human knowledge is encodable in streams of zeroes and ones—philosophically, that's very hard to swallow. In effect, the whole world is made to seem computable. This generates a kind of tunnel vision, where the only problems that seem legitimate are problems that can be put on a computer. There is a whole world of real problems, of human problems, which is essentially ignored."

Back to the home

One of the surprising happenings of the electronic age could be a reversal of the trend stimulated by the industrial revolution to move populations to the cities. Since it will now be possible to communicate so effectively without commuting, more and more people may choose to refocus their lives on their homes, and move their homes away from congestion. They can work, learn, and enjoy increasing leisure without the discomfort and expense of traveling into the urban crush. Continental Illinois Bank and Control Data Corporation, among others, are allowing some of their people to work at home. With computers many jobs can be performed as well or better in surroundings more comfortable than crowded office spaces. Companies may also save on construction or rental costs. Opportunities for handicapped persons are increased.

Futurist John Naisbett questions whether people will be happy working at home, claiming, "The more technology we introduce into society, the more people will want to be with other people." Yet another best-selling futurist, Alvin Toffler, thinks that the lack of face-to-face contact on the job will rekindle the tradition of strong family life and deep community involvement. He believes that the "electronic cottage" will "touch off a renaissance among voluntary organizations."

There will be times, of course, when it will be necessary to assemble employees for face-to-face exchange, but these can be scheduled when convenient and are different from the daily ordeal with bus, train, or traffic congestion. Many conferences can even be held without meeting in one central place. Corporations as different as Ford, Atlantic Richfield, and Merrill Lynch have found that teleconferencing can reach more people with less expenditure and be satisfactory for many purposes.

For some people, in some situations, this movement can extend the choice of where to live. It can also increase the options of "flex-time," the practice of staggering hours rather than requiring all employees to begin and end their working days at the same time.

Homemakers are not being overlooked in the planned utilization of computers. Shopping can be conducted by viewing prospective purchases on the video screen and placing an order. Stock market information is available at all times. Microwave ovens can be equipped with television receivers offering recipes and instructional demonstrations. There will even be electronic discs, to be sewn on toddler's clothing, allowing parents to check the child's location in the neighborhood by pushing a button.

Whether employed in or out of the home, citizens of the electronic age should be able to enjoy increased meaningful leisure. For dedicated workaholics this will mean nothing. For other people, however, the new technologies should make it possible to devote less time to remunerative labor, allowing more opportunity for recreation and learning experiences. The possibilities for occupying those leisure hours will also be multiplied by the resources of the new media.

Economic dislocation

Electronic enthusiasts anticipate a new age where human services will be extended and drudgery will be turned over to machines. An accompanying result, however, is almost certain to be unemployment.

The movement to computerized automation means a shift from labor-intensive to capital-intensive industry. A single company may avoid firing employees by reducing its work force gradually through normal attrition and by becoming so competitive that a larger share of the market is won. Meanwhile, less far-sighted companies will be going out of business. Overall, a painful adjustment is inevitable.

Will growth in information industries take up the slack? In high tech companies there are a few highly skilled and highly paid specialists, but three-fourths of all employees are paid low wages and are subject to loss of jobs if manufacturing is transferred abroad—a likely prospect. Thousands of middle-class workers face an indefinite period of unemployment with a sharp decline in income as the only long-term prospect. The electronic age is bringing with it severe economic dislocation. To date there is little evidence of national planning to meet the crisis.

Trade-off risks

The severity of two other previously identified dangers is less clear. Know-it-all computers can be a threat to privacy but individuals may, if we choose, have some control over input concerning our personal lives. Society has also demonstrated the ability to offer basic protection of privacy in the use of telephones and mail. Some defenses against errors in credit ratings have already been legislated. A person refused credit may demand to know the reason for the refusal, along with the name of the agency providing a negative report. The agency's information may then be challenged and the customer has the right to insert an explanation in the record. The Warner Amex Company has instituted its own "Privacy Code" in an effort to deal with this issue through self-regulation.

In the long run we must take into account the fact that the same computer that correlates attitudes and expenditures can perform important services, such as locating organ donors for persons critically in need. We are offered a trade-off—the risk of losing some privacy for access to new opportunities.

The threat from hackers, or computer code-crackers, offers a similar trade-off. It is possible for either adult criminals or juvenile pranksters to break into a computer system and disrupt it. This was especially easy before the danger became so obvious and safeguards were installed. It may never be possible to construct a completely foolproof process, but the same teenagers who are applying their brilliance to cracking a system may devise improved means for protecting it.

Christians face changes

Although the first Christians "turned the world upside down," their modern counterparts are better known for defending the old than for welcoming the new. Our congregations are unlikely to be in the forefront of technological explorations.

Some attention is being given by churches to the use of computers, principally in administration. They can store financial records, print quarterly giving statements, and facilitate the reporting of trends in income and attendance. They can adapt form letters to individual circumstances and supply mailing labels for selected groups within a congregation. By classifying interests and abilities of members they can help in the enlistment of volunteers and the formation of study groups. The preparation of bulletins, newsletters, and sermons is expedited. With careful planning and exploration of available software, the same instruments can be used for education as for administration. Students accustomed to having access to the most helpful media in their secular schools notice the absence of such devices in religious education.

In one project testing the field of electronic communication for church use, the Lutheran Church in America supplies a weekly electronic newsletter to The Source, a computer communication data base. The service contains news about the world of religion and special sections on religion and technology, and is accessible to anyone with a personal computer connected to the telephone.

Several denominations have used teleconferencing for national events, linking groups assembled in various locations. Depending on the number and geographical distribution of participants, this process can save travel costs, although it is not inexpensive.

Prospects for extended use by churches of teleconferencing are dim if experiences with an older medium are indicative. Telephone conference calls have been possible for many years but most religious leaders seldom tap this resource, electing instead to travel great distances to confer with small committees. Time and money could be saved by more frequent use of conference calls. Facial expressions, gestures, and body language add little to conversations with close acquaintances. Deliberation among such people need not be inhibited by the use of electronic devices.

Congregations have used the combination of telephone and recordings for "Dial a Prayer" services. This is basically an impersonal contact, inferior to invitations to dial a number staffed by a trained counselor. One variation is the telephone tape library, offering access to hundreds of instructional tapes listed in newspaper ads.

Videotape may prove to be one of the most useful educational tools, and churches are experimenting with its use. As is so often the case, however, commercial and secular agencies have produced and distributed a wide range of cassettes while religious leaders were only contemplating possible developments. A few independent producers and at least one denomination, the Southern Baptists, have taken more initiative than most other religious groups.

Southern Baptists are also involved in satellite distribution, as are the Church of Jesus Christ of Latter Day Saints (Mormons), the U.S. Catholic Conference, and a few other denominations on experimental bases. All are confronted with financial problems. In general, the multiplication of public channels through cable and satellite is likely to widen the gap between evangelical-independent and mainline church involvement in media. Additional access, especially on a commercial basis, will multiply the number of sectarian programs. By 1984 CBN (Christian Broadcasting Network) included 3900 cable systems and PTL (Praise the Lord) had access to 825 systems. A different type of operation, the National Christian Network (NCN), was established to make TV time available to a broader spectrum of religious broadcasters, provided they would refrain from soliciting funds on the air. Few mainline churches, however, have taken advantage of the opportunity.

One of the most interesting experiments is the formation, in at least four countries, of private corporations to distribute to stations and networks entertainment programs affirming traditional values. In the U.S., Dominion Satellite Network (DSN) has filed applications for 30 low-power TV stations in major markets and plans later to cover the entire country with satellite direct-to-home broadcasting. Founder-chairman Robert W. Johnson believes networks have become vulnerable because their competition with each other has led to neglect of the public. He says, "Nationwide research shows there is an audience large enough to attract national advertisers for wholesome family programming that upholds Judeo-Christian ethics, and that's what ours will do."

The Public Broadcasting System offers, in many respects, an alternative to commercial networks, but it does little for religious broadcasting. Wary of sectarian competition, PBS nationally has nearly excluded religion from its programming. Since many PBS outlets have ties with state universities, there is also fear of violating the shibboleth of separation between church and state.

In the seventies many religious groups experimented with cable, becoming involved in local origination and public access programming. Response was often disappointing because of the small number of early subscribers. The time and effort required for production also reduced some of the initial enthusiasm. As a result many opportunities for "narrowcasting" remain largely unexplored.

All sorts of congregational ventures could be undertaken by cable and telephone—instruction classes, stewardship campaigns, forums on current issues. Instead of drawing people out of their homes so often and fragmenting relationships, the church could become more of a force for strengthening family ties. Programming for such specialized purposes could almost never be placed on over-the-air stations, but there is no reason why it could not be scheduled on a public access cable channel.

The addition of low power TV outlets to the list of religious stations will not necessarily increase the audience for such broadcasts; it may simply scatter it over more channels. Commercialism on religious stations may also be especially offensive, as in this actual announcement:

> God has blessed George's Hair Design with talented, loving people. Tell your friends. We welcome you in the name of Jesus. You'll be blessed!

Such practices demonstrate that more religious channels will not necessarily increase outreach and influence of the church. But past misuse is no excuse for abdication from future responsibility. Before all opportunity is lost for more effective Christian involvement in electronic media, new and old, it is important for us to analyze previous efforts and give thought to what might be done to strengthen our impact on public communication. This will be the thrust of our next section.

PART TWO

Ventures in Media Ministry

The Religious Ghetto: Claims and Counterclaims

Church broadcasts are often described as a religious ghetto because they are so confined to early Sunday morning, at least on major commercial stations. At this point in the week they do the least damage to a station's ratings and most people are still asleep anyway. The ghetto image also reflects the belief that the regular listener-viewers of such programs are a small minority of the population.

Accurate information concerning the audience for religious broadcasts is difficult to obtain, partly because results from the few surveys attempted are so often misinterpreted. This was true even of the two-year study commissioned by a coalition of 39 religious agencies, conducted by the Annenberg School of Communications at the University of Pennsylvania and the Gallup Organization, and completed in 1984.

Incorporating what I term "media mania math," reports of the study indicated that the audience for religious television is inconsequential and radically different from the general population. These conclusions come out of a Nielsen-Arbitron orientation versus a biblical lost-sheep approach.

There is evidence that the *regular* audience for television programs *ordinarily* presented under *church auspices* is small in *comparison* with the figures for prime-time entertainment shows.

The italics suggest four corrections to be made in this typical misconstruction:

- The *regular* audience for religious television is not all-important. In fact, occasional viewers may present the best opportunity for media contact.

- Programs *ordinarily* presented do not indicate the range of possibilities. The Annenberg-Gallup study concentrated on a two-week period during which mainline programs were more ordinary than attractive.

- By confining its statistical analysis to programs sponsored by *church agencies* the Annenberg-Gallup study disregarded network and syndicated productions such as *Jesus of Nazareth* and *The Scarlet and the Black*. The study thus overlooked an important element in audience interest.

- Rating *comparisons* are almost irrelevant for our purposes. An audience which may be small in terms of commercial television may be either large in comparison with the numbers assembled in church gatherings or significant in lost sheep mathematics.

Nor is the audience for religious television as singular or as atypical as commonly reported. Such terms as "tend to," "by and large," and "more likely" obscure the fact that most viewers of religious television are much like nonviewers. Most viewers have nominal denominational ties but so do most nonviewers. Age differences are cited, but 70.8% of the viewers are between 30 and 65 years, compared with 65% of nonviewers. The importance placed on religion is another alleged difference between the two groups; it is true that nearly all viewers of religious TV regard religion as important, but 80% of nonviewers also regard religion as either important or very important.

Because of these and similar questionable comparisons, observations from the Annenberg-Gallup study concerning prospects for media evangelism are generally distorted, but this will be discussed in Chapter 8.

Stripped of statistical aberrations, studies indicate a substantial potential audience for religious television. With occasional exceptions, however, the actual audience falls short of what could be expected.

Why is this? How influential are religious broadcasts? Do they strengthen or weaken congregational ties? Do they drain funds from churches? There are great differences among the programs being aired. What are the advantages and disadvantages of various approaches?

Traditional indoctrination

Early religious broadcasters relied chiefly on the method familiar to them—preaching. Whether the time period was an hour, half an hour, 15 minutes, or even 5 minutes, the devotional format was used and talk was the central element, perhaps surrounded by hymns.

These attempts are dismissed by most media specialists as inappropriate for broadcasting, but they have served a purpose. They have meant much to shut-ins and the occasional, lukewarm listener-viewers who happened to tune in at a time when they were ready to hear a particular message. Such programs can also be defended on the basis that it is better for the clergy to do well what they are trained to do than to play roles for which they lack credibility. This approach, however, has limitations.

One of the most overlooked passages in Scripture is Eccl. 5:2, "Be not rash with your mouth, nor let your heart be hasty to utter a word before God, for God is in heaven, and you upon earth; therefore let your words be few." Beginning with Paul, Christian theologians have contradicted this admonition.

We have tried to conquer the world with a verbal barrage. We have concentrated on didactic, intellectually-oriented indoctrination, in contrast with Jesus' emphasis on action and story.

This is partly because of our heritage of confessions and catechisms. The verbal question-and-answer formula suited the purpose of the reformers to convey precise religious knowledge. Both Protestants and Roman Catholics adopted catechisms as weapons in their struggle. What success did they have? Not much, according to Jesuit scholar Thomas H. Clancy. When questioned in 1581 about their reasons for not going to church, some Protestant citizens of Leipzig replied that "the Turk and the Pope are not doing us any harm." This answer, says Clancy, "reveals the weakness of the catechetical and dialectical approach; it apparently works best when the enemy or enemies are in plain view and constitute a present danger. . . . Historians agree that the catechetical method of religious instruction worked best in a hostile or at least an unfriendly environment."

In our modern churches we often wonder why young people become inactive immediately after completing a series of instruction classes. It may well be because we are still attempting to communicate the faith in too abstract a manner. We have even deflated the perfectly good word "preach" until one dictionary definition reads, "to convey moral or religious advice in a tiresome or obtrusive manner." Someone has noted that the Lord's Prayer contains 56 words, the Ten Commandments 297. An average sermon may run to 3500 words.

Several years ago Lutheran churches of the world celebrated an anniversary of an important historical document, the Augsburg Confession. Events were planned and countless articles were written. Afterward there was a gathering to evaluate the results of the year. One church sent a representative with instructions to say "as clearly as possible that *nothing* had happened!" Many laypersons from other churches undoubtedly agreed with the conclusion that there had been insufficient translation of the medieval document into meaning for today. The church often appears to be confronting an open society with a closed system.

Words, words, words

The difficulty Christians often have in communicating our faith verbally may be due, in part, to dependence on print. Martin Luther is recognized for his use of print, but he regarded the gospel as primarily a spoken word, not a book. Even the fact that the Gospels had to be written was a weakness, according to Luther, "a great breach and a quenching of the spirit." He had no intention of replacing the spoken word with the written, and insisted, "The gospel is, and cannot be other than, the account or the story of Christ."

The philosopher Plato had reservations about words, especially written words. In the *Phaedrus* he argued that the new arrival of writing would revolutionize culture for the worse. He suggested that it would "substitute reminiscence for thought, and mechanical learning for the true dialectic of the living quest for truth by discourse and conversation." Ironically, all we know of Plato has been communicated to us through written words.

Our western academic system has put such emphasis on words, and especially on written abstractions, that oral communication with nonprofessionals has been handicapped. Theologians are aware of this. Reinhold Neibuhr, speaking in a Union Seminary chapel service, once expressed the hope that graduates of that institution "would be fumigated of their esoteric vocabularies by the winds of common sense" after leaving the seminary. The eloquent statement from John 1:14 is revised: the Word becomes words and floats above us, full of abstraction and ambiguity.

The trouble is that professors and students alike lose their ability to distinguish between technical jargon and living language. The layman Myles Horton, founder and longtime leader of a community of socially concerned persons, has recalled an illustration of this. Many years ago, without the usual academic credentials, he applied for admission to Union Seminary and, to his surprise, was admitted. Quickly he established a relationship with the young Reinhold Niebuhr, who allowed him to register for two graduate seminars. After the first session Horton asked to withdraw, saying he hadn't understood a thing. This caused Niebuhr to question other students who admitted they were also in the dark. Niebuhr then asked Horton to return and raise his hand when something was said which he could not understand. Perhaps the interactive possibilities of the new media will offer a similar opportunity for feedback but, in the past, many religious broadcasters have been speaking on a different wavelength from the one to which their listener-viewers were tuned.

Neither simple nor obscure

Recognition of the verbiage problem leads easily to the wrong conclusion: make it simple. This temptation is particularly strong in a medium about which the interviewer Dick Cavett could say, "Only a blockhead would try to be cerebral on television." Cavett is able to guide interviewees into thoughtful discussions, but he obviously believes that being labeled an intellectual will limit his audience to the minority of persons who regard this as an advantage.

Many Christian truths are far from simple, but profundity is not the same as obscurity. And just because a truth is profound does not mean it is abstract. The understanding of grace as unconditional love can be communicated in very concrete form. This is often overlooked by critics who dismiss electronic media for the wrong reasons. One pastor-editor of an ecumenical weekly was disparaging "religionists . . . mesmerized by electronics" and church bodies spending large sums "because they believe this is the way to teach the ignorant eternal truths." He asked, "But can abstract truths be taught this easily?"

Who said our scriptural heritage was abstract? The prophets did not think so. Moses demanded, "Let my people go!" and the children of Israel traced their beginnings to delivery from bondage in Egypt. Our Lord spoke more often in concrete than in abstract terms. In actions the Word became flesh.

In a sense, of course, all words are abstractions. The word *lily* is no more an actual flower than the word *reconciliation* is an actual event, but the second is surely more abstract than the first. Communication requires movement back and forth across the various levels. More abstract elements are built on relatively concrete bases. The reader or listener can then move from a simple, understandable image to an abstract proposition and back again.

When Christians have trouble expressing their faith through modern media, the problem may not lodge entirely in the media. It is true that broadcasting is strong in terms of the visual, the concrete, action, relationships, and the immediate. Our difficulty with the media may reflect a weakness in all of our communicative attempts. According to one tongue-in-cheek observation, if the Acts of the Apostles were being written today they would be called the Resolutions of the Apostles. Our experience with public media may say something about what we should be doing in our overall mission.

Sub-Christian adaptation

Evangelical independents have not felt hampered by the nature of the electronic media. There was a time when their broadcasts also contained mostly traditional preaching, but in recent years they have tried many different approaches in efforts to increase the size of their audiences. Today the most common form for the most widely circulated programs (such as the "700 Club" and the "PTL Club") is the interview-variety program, modeled on the "Tonight Show." Even televised worship services, like the "Hour of Power," include interviews with guest stars and performances by them. Producers of these programs honestly admit that since broadcasting is primarily an entertainment medium they are simply taking into account the predisposition of potential listener-viewers.

To attract customers, advertisers claim their products will give people what they want: enjoyment, health, security, popularity. They search for some real or contrived characteristic of a soap, perfume, automobile, or over-the-counter drug which can be glamorized to hook potential buyers. Some popular religious broadcasters follow the same strategy. What do people want most—peace of mind? Then let's focus on selected parts of Scripture which will seem to offer this, disregarding all of the contrasting passages. Audiences are built by offering simple solutions to difficult problems, easy answers to complex questions.

The dictatorship of listeners

This is not a new temptation for religious leaders. While independent broadcasters must attract thousands of people and raise millions of dollars to stay on the air, preachers in ordinary parishes feel the need to hold hundreds of members and collect thousands of dollars to support the congregation's work. Even without financial constraints there is the natural desire to please rather than to offend. The German theologian Helmut Thielicke warns against "the dictatorship of listeners" which results in a "homiletical lullaby":

> If the preacher makes himself dependent upon the given hearers in his congregation, he will be sucked into a vicious

circle. Old people love sentiment and feeling, and they want no problems; they hardly know what to make of it if one tells them what the gospel can mean for the great conflicts of life and the bitter ensnarements of passion.

Audiences for most religious broadcasts include a number of elderly church members with little formal education. Among them are some of the finest, most deeply committed persons in the Christian community, but their number also includes many who want only to be spiritually sedated. Religious broadcasters may cater to this easily identifiable group.

Pat Robertson of the "700 Club" adapts to his audience partly by claiming to be an expert in a surprising range of fields. He has advised his followers when to store soybeans and whether to invest in gold or land. He connects current events with obscure passages in the prophets and the book of Revelation. He predicted that the Soviet Union would invade Israel in 1982.

Mainline church leaders are also susceptible to sub-Christian adaptation when they attempt to communicate through the mass media. A classic example was the spot announcement distributed by the interdenominational Religion in American Life campaign, "Bring your troubles to church—and leave them there." Bring your troubles to church? Of course. But you may acquire some new ones, if you pay attention, along with partnership in dealing with both old and new ones. One congregation pasted over the exit from the sanctuary a more authentic sign, "Servant's Entrance."

One denomination produced an announcement portraying Christ's meeting with the woman taken in adultery. It concluded with the words, "Neither do I condemn you," omitting "go, and do not sin again" (John 8:11). In trying to express our faith through brief segments we face special dangers of oversimplification and distortion. Spot announcements influence chiefly through constant, nearly hypnotic repetition of brand names, connected with dubious attributes of products. One advertising executive has leveled with sponsors: "If you can't afford frequency, don't bother

advertising." Church-produced announcements are never granted frequency of exposure and the entire process makes it ex-
tremely difficult for such productions to have positive results.
Later we will take note of rare exceptions.

Parts of the whole

So religious broadcasters are selective in their treatment of
biblical themes. They emphasize the upbeat. Is that so bad? Robert Schuller admits that he does not generally present the whole
gospel in his telecasts, depending on congregations to supplement
his partial presentations. He also defends accusations of blandness
by explaining that it is impossible to be controversial without
offending people. Jesus was not unaware of this fact, but it did
not prevent him from entering into controversy. He, however,
was not intent on building a crystal cathedral.

It is questionable whether a preacher or teacher can convey
the whole gospel in a single session. Nearly all presentations are
partial. But the same preacher, or same program, with continued
exposure week after week, should be able to round out the description of faith as something more than a magical formula for
pleasure. The cross may be a hurdle to TV ratings and money
raising, but it is also an elevator lifting troubled human beings
out of anxiety and despair.

Political evangelism

Many of the so-called evangelicals emphasize old, cherished
values: patriotism, law and order, clear opposition to homosexuality and abortion. Ultraconservatives are attracted by preachers
who call for the banning of books, criticize public education, and
even oppose child-abuse laws.

There was a time when evangelical independents deliberately
avoided all reference to politics. Rex Humbard once said, "I don't
fight anybody. If I ever got into politics I'd be like a blacksmith
pulling a tooth. It would be a bloody mess."

Other religious broadcasters, however, have moved in the opposite direction, going so far as to endorse some candidates and
oppose others. Conservative religion is merged with conservative

politics and preachers promote their own definition of what it means to be conservative. A particular brand of Christianity is depicted as engaged in a life-and-death struggle with atheistic socialism. On this basis money can be raised both for the broadcasters and for far-right political organizations.

Preferred candidates may be selected solely on the basis of their positions on single issues, such as their past opposition to transfer of the Panama Canal or support of increased military spending. At a time when independent evangelicals were advocating U.S. retention of the Canal Zone, I was hearing overseas Christians warn American churches that our country would lose moral credibility if we held onto this piece of distant land. More recently, European Christians, who have experienced war's devastation and are challenging their own governments to take peace initiatives, cannot understand how American religious groups can favor armament buildups.

Opponents on the "hit lists" may be sincere Christians, deeply committed to expressing God's will in dealing with a broad range of governmental responsibilities. Like other Christians, political candidates may have different viewpoints even about such dilemmas as abortion legislation and prayer in schools, but the far right sets its own black-and-white standards. Unfortunately, these standards often overlook such clear biblical precepts as concern for the poor and disadvantaged. The image of the Christian church emerging from many independent telecasts is one of self-righteousness, lacking in compassion.

Personality cults

It is no coincidence that religious telecasts with the highest ratings feature individuals. Speakers often encourage this development in both subtle and obvious ways. Oral Roberts encourages constituents to write directly to him. Twenty thousand letters are received daily and a computerized process turns out responses appearing to have received personal attention.

When Robert Schuller advocates his method of "possibility thinking," he often cites his own experiences as examples of how to be successful. Approaching completion of his crystal cathedral, he said, "We are close to one of the greatest success stories of the century." Soliciting 3000 gifts of $1,500 each, he gave prospective donors a special address which would speed each check to a desk in his private office, where he would see it personally.

The influence of Christian personalities is not a modern phenomenon; Peter and Paul attracted crowds. Protestant denominations were founded by followers of strong leaders. Thomas Clancy of Loyola University has speculated:

> It is mind-boggling to think of Luther on the tube. There is no doubt that he would be a hit. Nor is there any doubt that he would be more fiercely attacked than any of the current television preachers. Are they vulgar? Luther was even more vulgar, and he even had a little corps of Mike Wallaces to record in his "Table Talk" those of his indiscretions that he left out of his sermons. Are television preachers building personality cults? Luther constantly complained of the same thing, but confessed that there was little he could do about it.

Luther, however, could not be accused of exploiting his popularity to raise money for his own pet projects, nor of luring people away from the gathered community of believers. These two charges are leveled regularly against the so-called electronic church, and facts are often mixed with fiction.

Religious commercialism

Electronic evangelists do raise large sums of money. Revenues for Pat Robertson and Jimmy Swaggart have exceeded 60 million dollars per year, and Jerry Falwell projects receipts of 2 billion dollars by 1987.

The escalating cost for appearing on television requires more and more income from audiences. Billy Graham, who uses TV only sparingly and limits the time devoted to financial appeals on his programs, has cautioned: "There is a danger when TV preachers begin to beg too frequently and too fervently. Money is a *means*: it must never be the *message*." Having watched a program in which the speaker spent nearly half his time pleading for donations, Graham says, "Such preachers bring reproach to the Gospel, and damage all other religious TV programs."

Periodically the electronic ventures face financial crises. Early in 1984 Jimmy Swaggart pleaded with viewers to sit down and write checks because he was faced with three million dollars of unpaid bills.

At about the same time Jerry Falwell devoted an entire program to repetitious, blatant appeals for monthly contributions of $100, $25, or $10. No other type of sponsor would be allowed to present an hour-long commercial broadcast.

The appeals used to raise large sums from listener-viewers are sometimes as misleading as commercial advertising. Evangelists solicit funds to help reach the unchurched but, when accused of attracting members away from churches, claim that most of their listener-viewers are active in congregations. The "700 Club" has used a commercial in which Christ is portrayed urging to "go and preach the Gospel," whereupon an announcer comments that this commission can be fulfilled today through radio and television, but that this is possible "only through your support of the '700 Club.'"

Stewardship on TV is often reduced to a celestial slot machine. Such passages as "Seek ye first the kingdom of God . . . and all these things shall be added unto you" (Matt. 6:33 KJV) are distorted into a promise that anyone who supports a program with money will prosper financially. Examples are cited of low-income persons who risked their rent money by making a contribution and then found a windfall. Rev. Ike, a New York religious entrepreneur, carries this to its ultimate absurdity. All you need to do, he says, it imagine yourself in a desired situation and it will happen. If you want a car, you'll get it. He can sound sincere because he has 20 Rolls Royces.

Rex Humbard once addressed a delinquent contributor on the air: "Dear Thomas, last week I knelt at the prayer altar to pray for every member in the Prayer Key Family Book, and I wanted to pray for you . . . but your name was not there." Not since Tetzel in the 16th century has so crass a threat been employed.

It may well be that most of the money given to the electronic church would not find its way into denominational budgets anyway. If it could, however, a much larger percentage would be devoted to mission and reducing world hunger. The more affluent religious broadcasters attempt to address such needs, but only after paying huge bills for production and air time.

The commercialism of religious broadcasting also creates an unfortunate image of the Christian church. It reinforces the cynic's view that the church is interested only in financial contributions.

Spectators or followers

A major objection to the electronic church is the option it offers for persons to become mere spectators of religious variety shows instead of cross-bearing followers. Television evangelists are accused of luring people away from the more demanding—and more fulfilling—relationships in a gathered community of believers. Personally, I have never believed that religious broadcasts keep many people away from church. Absentees may use such programs as excuses for nonattendance, but if their receivers were broken they would find another reason to stay home. Anyone who has made evangelism calls in homes knows that there is no limit to the number of excuses contrived for absence from worship services; broadcasting is only a particularly convenient and respectable one.

Whenever the charge that television reduces church membership is made publicly, there are indignant responses. After William F. Fore, head of the Communication Commission of the National Council of Churches, had expressed in *TV Guide* his fear that the electronic church "provides an easy and convenient substitute for face-to-face church attendance," he received a flood of letters, including the following:

> Five years ago I was saved from my sins and entered into a personal relationship with Jesus Christ, because of the PTL Club. I am currently very active in my local church, Word of Faith. Many of our church members, although they had

a religious background, came to know Jesus Christ because of a television ministry.

Some people do find electronic evangelism to be more attractive than the ministry of their local church. We have identified some of the reasons for this; there are others as well.

Added attractions

The sheer audacity of some clerical entrepreneurs has its own appeal. Pat Robertson has developed a cable network offering round-the-clock programming of old movie greats, game shows, sports, and news, along with his "700 Club" productions and soap opera "Another Life." The network is operated commercially, claiming to offer a wholesome alternative to the sex-and-violence orientation of the three major networks. The network headquarters at Virginia Beach, Virginia, occupies a 387-acre complex that includes a 22-million-dollar production building and an adjoining graduate-level university in communications and other fields.

Robert Schuller does not apologize for splurging 20 million dollars on his cathedral in a world full of needy people. Instead, he insists that beauty in art and architecture plays its part in uplifting the human spirit, and moves on to his next plan. He now hopes to establish a national chain of retreat centers for troubled people. He intends that eventually no major city will be far away from a place where persons with broken marriages or broken lives may go for solace and strength. If mainline churches were as innovative as Robertson and Schuller in their projections, denominational funding might be less difficult.

The electronic church also attracts through its emphases on joy and caring. Mainline congregational worship has been characterized more by solemnity than by joy. The columnist Erma Bombeck wrote about a smiling child whose mother jerked him around and, in a loud whisper, said, "Stop that grinning! You're in church!" Bombeck asked what such children must think when "We sing, 'Make a joyful noise unto the Lord,' while our faces reflect the sadness of one who has just buried a rich aunt who left everything to her pregnant hamster." She adds that God "had to have a sense of humor to have created the likes of us."

It is vital that Christians not lose sight of the cross, but we are followers of the risen Christ, and Jesus' words to Mary Magdalene outside the open tomb are applicable: "Why are you crying?" At their best, the electronic evangelists may be offering a partial corrective for the image of the church as a despondent collection of perpetual mourners.

Religious broadcasters prod mainline congregations from another direction. With their 800 numbers and their staffs of volunteer counselors, the electronic evangelists at least appear to invite personal contact with listener-viewers. Some of this concern is undoubtedly connected with the need for contributions, and computer processing makes the contact less than truly personal, but there is still an important symbolism in the invitation. In how many congregations is there a 24-hour opportunity to air concerns with the assurance that fellow-members stand ready to offer assistance? Instead of complaining about competition from the electronic church, perhaps a congregation should concentrate on becoming the caring community it ought to be. Then the partially contrived communal appeal of the TV evangelists would suffer by comparison.

Elitist criticism

Most programs from the religious ghetto have theological weaknesses. Friends in the parish ministry report to me that religious instruction is an increasingly difficult process because of misunderstandings created by electronic evangelists. We must admit, however, that the level of biblical knowledge in our congregations has never been very high. Are the present religious broadcasts harmful? Or are they simply less worthwhile than discriminating believers would prefer?

Professor Robert M. Price, writing in the *Christian Century*, warns against being snobs in our criticism of the electronic church. He is certain "that mass market faith is a trivialization of Christ, even an opiate of the people." But he is realistic enough to recognize that "one just cannot expect everybody to understand or heed a call to radical discipleship," and regards such a demand as elitist. He believes, therefore, we must admit "that, just as people have different levels of appreciation and taste (in food and music, for example), so it is with religious sensibilities." He concludes that all Christians must confess the faith delivered to them but not be overly troubled about the faith of others.

I would rather say that different tastes may be recognized without outright condemnation but with the hope of enrichment. A parent may go along at times with a child's choice of hamburgers, french fries, and candy in preference to not eating anything, but there can also be effort made toward acquiring taste for a more nutritious diet. Sugar is not the only seasoning. There is biblical precedent for applying salt, provided it has not lost its saltness.

Toward Better 6
Communication

It is no secret that major denominations have made little impact on the mass media in America. Communication specialists within these denominations have disparaged both the content-oriented presentation of traditionalists and the media adaptations of independent evangelicals. Most mainline efforts, however, have also fallen short because they have sold out to theoretical fads at the expense of sound theology. While independents were distorting theology to conform to Madison Avenue precepts of how to attract an audience, mainline innovators were diluting theology to fit their current psychological and sociological leanings. Content became irrelevant; all attention was focused on form and process.

Civilization in reverse

Religious broadcasters became enamored with a theory popularized by media producer Tony Schwartz. His "resonance principle" treats people like computerized zombies. We are exposed to so many sensory impressions that we neither analyze nor respond to them immediately. We store them until a later time when they are evoked for us in a patterned way by new stimuli. That is, when someone pushes the right button in our sensory apparatus, we respond in terms of previously accumulated suggestions. Applying this to political advertising, Schwartz says its purpose is "to surround the voter with proper auditory and visual stimuli: to evoke the reaction you want for him, that is, his voting for a specific candidate."

Schwartz became a guru of popular culture with the television commercial he created for Lyndon Johnson's campaign against Barry Goldwater. The spot showed a little girl in a field, counting petals on a daisy. As her count reached 10, the visual motion was frozen and the viewer heard a countdown. When this reached zero viewers saw a nuclear explosion and heard President Johnson say, "These are the stakes to make a world in which all God's children can live or go into the darkness. Either we must love each other or we must die." As the screen went to black, white lettering appeared, "On November 3 vote for President Johnson."

The spot created a huge controversy, with Republicans claiming it accused Senator Goldwater of being trigger-happy. Actually, of course, there was no reference to Goldwater, but he had stated previously that he supported the use of tactical atomic weapons and the commercial evoked fears related to this. Schwartz explained, "We are not concerned with getting things across to people as much as out of people."

Some religious broadcasters followed Schwartz and McLuhan in attempting to communicate by discarding rational thought in favor of a barrage of impressions attempting only to stimulate some kind of response. Michael J. Arlen, writing in the *New Yorker,* saw this trend as an attempted reversal of the civilizing process. He said,

> We aren't going to want to do without logic—intuitive, deductive, analytical, linear, call it what you will. After all, logic, brains, intellect, sustained formal thought are how we splendid, wonderful people got to be so splendid and wonderful in the first place, and when a philosopher-king like McLuhan starts saying things like, "The way you react to them (television and computers) is what is important, not what is in them or on them," it's hard to forget that the first thing boring old Gutenberg printed was the Bible and the first thing television gave us was Uncle Miltie—and, on present evidence, there doesn't seem to be any very pressing basis for tossing out the first because of the second.

Post-Christian rambling

Religious broadcasting disciples of Tony Schwartz conclude that there is no point in attempting to communicate through the media anything as substantial or perplexing as the "stumbling block" of the gospel. Serious concern for meaning and purpose is ruled out; we need only expose people to impressions, encourage the asking of questions and the sharing of experiences. The outcome is likely to be a post-Christian rambling which retains almost no significant element of biblical faith.

This approach may be perfectly appropriate for persons who do not claim to be Christian. I respect Arnold Toynbee for his open advocacy of a post-Christian religion. As a historian he was dismayed by the international conflicts related to religious differences and he believed that, if the world is to survive, a new religion must evolve. He thought this was reasonable because he had concluded that the permanent essence of all higher religions is the same—love versus selfishness. He believed that the new religion should take science into account but could retain the ethical precepts common to nearly all faiths.

There have been many broadcasts produced under the auspices of mainline churches which have reflected, consciously or unconsciously, Toynbee's point of view. One reason why mainline broadcasting has received limited support is because so few programs have represented the core of mainstream Christian faith. Some could even be regarded as authentic Zen Buddhism, operating entirely on the basis of "indirect communication," with the only goal being self-discovery. Lutheran theologian James Burtness has challenged this trend toward a Christless church, saying, "Somebody somewhere has to name the name of Jesus or the jig is up; it's all over and we're in the business then of helping people to be religious which is not a hell of a lot better than helping them to be moral and which has little to do with the Christian faith."

If this sounds too much like the fanatics who plant "Jesus saves" signs at sharp turns on mountain highways, a quote from theologian Paul Tillich may be in order. Tillich tried as hard as anyone to interpret Christian faith in contemporary terms, but he acknowledged the necessity of preserving the vertical along with the horizontal element in theology. He said, "There is a gap between the divine and human, so that man needs more than a midwife like Socrates who brings out of us what we already have within us; something new must come from outside. The Savior or the Christ must come."

Reference to the name of Jesus is not simply a shibboleth but recognition of the fact that in Christ God has intersected human life in a way that transforms ordinary inclinations, values, and securities, showing us who we can become and how we can walk with him beside us. When we downplay this central feature of the faith, we replace the gospel with a psychological fad.

Electronic dilution of the faith is not limited to the United States. Peter Ackroyd in the *London Times* reviewed a British TV program, "Credo," which, he said, "for want of a better word we must call a 'religious' series," and "unveiled God as an aging hippy." According to the program, Ackroyd claimed, "God is really, then, an Ongoing Process symbolizing Sharing, Freedom, Permissiveness, a sort of cosmic *Oh Calcutta!*" The producers, he said, "by grasping all of the cliches which emerged in the Sixties and Seventies, are in the unenviable position of middle-aged men trying desperately to join a parade which has not only passed by but has also disbanded." For them, he wrote, God "is still a benign Father Christmas; they have merely taken off the white robes, and replaced them with a flowered shirt and medallion."

What I am saying is less an indictment than a confession. I have served on policymaking bodies responsible for approving expenditures for projects of dubious value. We have sometimes been too modest in our expectations. The Christian church today does not include a host of creative artists—they may have been driven away by fundamentalism and pietism. So when capable writers and producers undertake a project on behalf of a denomination, the tendency is to give them as free a rein as possible. The results can be "good shows" lacking any distinctively Christian element.

Ironically, avoiding the stumbling block of the gospel does not necessarily gain the attention of "outsiders." Theologian Rosemary Haughton writes, "The secular is just as much an idol as the God who is dead. Christians are busy burying the transcendent while the post-Christian generation . . . openly avows a hunger for the experience of God."

Process: another one-legged stool

Recognizing the importance of communicating the faith but questioning the role of media in that task, current broadcasting theory focuses on process and interaction. Genuine communication is not one-directional but circular; mere *transmission* of information is not enough. By the same token, an effort to avoid all instruction and simply draw everything out of listener-viewers can be called *derivation* and is equally one-directional; it simply reverses the direction. The message-confined approach is represented by a hypodermic needle—inject the truth into a passive recipient. The media-diluted approach is more like a sales pitch— find out how the prospects feel and cater to their wants.

To correct these narrow views, communication can be described as a process: interaction among people attempting to relate to one another. This concept, however, can be another one-legged stool; it cannot stand alone. Of course communication is a process, as is nearly every human effort and relationship. But communication is a multidimensional experience which must take into account message or content, media or form, and process or interactive context. Process without message is like a rocket lost in space. Message in media without process never achieves orbit. Any attempt to communicate the Christian faith must take into account the expression of that faith in content, the integrity of that expression in form, and the vitality of that expression in communal exchange. Instead of transmission or derivation, Christian communication is more like incarnation. To limit attention to any one aspect of communication encourages distortion.

The drift is seductive. If process is all-important, whatever stimulates interaction is valid. It is not difficult to meet this criterion. The result can even be endowed with a touch of theological respectability by classifying it as preevangelism, preparing for a later step in communicating the gospel. Nearly every production can be defended on these grounds. The fact that similar stimuli could be provided by others without our investment is conveniently overlooked.

When message and media are dissolved in process, the authority of the transcendent is replaced by transcendental meditation. Instead of worshiping the Creator, human beings join an encounter group in a hot tub, engaging in dialog and drawing everything out of "growth experiences." The Holy Spirit is no more welcome than Banquo's ghost, but nearly everything else is interpreted as "spiritual." To ask the right question becomes the ultimate objective; with no hint of answers it is not surprising that this is "the age of anxiety." Without realizing it, there has been a drift into a post-Christian posture.

The process orientation uses a model suggested by the French sociologist Roger Mehl—the Genesis story of Jacob wrestling with a mysterious man throughout the night before the reunion with Esau. This encounter involves struggle for identity, for domination, or at least for survival. It has many attractive elements, but is only an isolated fragment in the biblical record of communication. On the following day Jacob was overwhelmed by Esau's welcome and said, "Truly to see your face is like seeing the face of God, with such favor have you received me" (Gen. 33:10). That reconciliation has features not suggested by the wrestling match.

Many other biblical events indicate the variety of communicative possibilities: the agony of Abraham believing he was commanded to kill his son, Nathan's confrontation with David over the murder of Uriah, the epic of Israel's liberation, the parables, the quiet revelation of the risen Lord to the two disciples on the road to Emmaus, the preaching at Pentecost—the list is unending, as is the range of ways in which human beings relate to one another and to God.

A mistake is made when anyone selects one way congenial to him or her and suggests that this is the only authentic style of communicating the gospel.

Cranial complexity

Communication cannot be forced into narrow molds because the human brain is such a complex system. It is more than a chemical computer, more wonderful than the latest electronic contraption. Neuroscientists are discovering enormously complicated interactions within the brain. "A lot of old theories about right brain and left brain are nonsense," according to Daniel Weinberger of the National Institute of Health. "Things are not as localized as we thought." Knowledge of the chemistry of human emotions is still in its infancy. Evidence from surgical probes, along with observation of different personalities and ways of thinking, has convinced scientists that no two brains are alike.

When human beings are recognized as being different from machines—to be programmed into a particular process—the comprehensive nature of communication may emerge. For Christians this requires careful consideration of message, media, and interactive context.

Preservation of message

It is not only in broadcasting that mainline churches often appear to be post-Christian. Many congregations have become either folk shrines or community clubs.

Members of the shrines take pride in beautiful, air-conditioned facilities, hosting baptisms and weddings (specialized funeral homes serve most of the deceased). Inactives outnumber regular worshipers; only on Christmas Eve and Easter morning does attendance reach capacity. Prayers become fervent in times of personal loss or danger and there is disillusionment when such appeals seem to be unproductive. Otherwise the faith of members appears to make little difference in their daily lives and they seldom turn to one another for support and consolation.

The community clubs may provide recreational opportunities: gymnasiums, athletic teams, and social organizations. They may also resemble service clubs, in that membership implies a degree of recognition along with expectation of regular attendance, although there is no enforcement comparable to Rotary, Kiwanis, or Lions. Good citizenship and moral character are extolled. The

Rotary motto, "He profits most who serves the best," may even be the substance of some sermons, with the preacher carefully avoiding contradictory evidence from the Scriptures. Benevolence projects, funded by token contributions, are undertaken.

Under such conditions it is not surprising that religious broadcasts often fall short of expressing authentic Christian faith. It is more surprising, perhaps, that some ecumenical programs take more prophetic stands than are heard from most pulpits. South Africa's outrageous treatment of Namibia has been documented; shipment of food to North Vietnam was reported; refugee resettlement has been advocated.

Media appeal tends to tilt ecumenical programming in the direction of prevailing social issues: alcoholism, world hunger, peace, drug abuse—the whole range of national and global problems. This is certainly a valid function, especially when the issues are being neglected in the public media or when there is a theological perspective on them. Churches even have the legitimate function to offer broadcasts performing strictly humanitarian services, just as we feed the starving without quoting Scripture.

Given the costs of broadcasting and our limited resources, however, some pointed questions must be asked. Are we contributing anything which could not be done as well—or better—by other agencies? Are we taking theological leadership or baptizing sociopolitical presuppositions? What proportion of our communication efforts are devoted to pursuing what committed believers regard as our central purposes? When the bulk of denominational media budgets is invested in peripheral projects, responsible leaders ask legitimately whether there is a better use for such funds—in either more direct service functions, such as feeding the hungry and relocating refugees, or in a more significant effort to communicate the gospel.

In recent years National Council producers have tried to present more programs in line with current denominational emphases. This attempt is hobbled, however, by the limited scope of interdenominational cooperation. Production funds, promotion, and follow-up are minimal. The constraints of denominational representation fragment all efforts. There is little substantive continuity and no possibility to establish authentic personalities whose faith could be communicated by contagion. This last restraint is an understandable reaction against the independent celebrity cults.

All of which makes it even more crucial for churches to devote available finances to performing our central task—sharing the most valuable resource entrusted to us, the gospel. This is even a social responsibility connected with our involvement in public media. We do not submit the claims of the Christian faith as the only vision of truth, but we offer them as a corrective for prevailing attitudes of a pseudoscientific culture. The news of the gospel is our peculiar contribution to an exchange essential for society.

The exclusion of a distinctively Christian message from much media planning is due partly to a misunderstanding of the nature of the gospel. The gospel is not primarily a statement inviting agreement or disagreement. It is more of a promise, "Come with me into a fulfilling adventure," or an assurance of unconditional love. Independent broadcasters have caught this idea in saying, "I love you, and God loves you too!"

Mother Teresa has said that whereas in India many are dying of hunger, in the United States people are dying of emotional starvation. Young people who are critical of formalism and tradition are searching for acceptance, belonging, and something worthy of trust and commitment.

The challenging reality is that the gospel should have all the appeal of the latest news dealing with exciting happenings. Yoshira Ishida, Japanese theologian, insists that the gospel is the "event of God's saving action" rather than "a set of good teachings and statements." He concedes that the message can be formulated into a set of propositions but maintains, "propositions themselves, however neat and persuasive, just do not save people." He contends that our mission as Christians is "being involved in this event of God's saving action; not a static word-oriented activity but rather a dynamic action-oriented communication. . . . God's saving event 'happens' in the midst of our physical, secular living. . . ." Such a dynamic, action-oriented communication should not be out of place in dynamic, action-oriented media.

Disclosure through media

One of the persistent misunderstandings concerning radio and television is the belief that everyone tunes only to programs featuring entertainment they like and ideas with which they agree. This is true of most listener-viewers, which is all that most advertisers care to know. But there is also a significant minority of people who are receptive to new experiences, who are on the lookout for new information related to their needs or goals, who may be challenged by positions sharply contrasting with their own and will even retain those ideas for later consideration.

Although this audience will not lead in the Nielsen figures at any one time, it is not always composed of the same people, and over a long enough period will include most of the population. This presents an unusual opportunity for Christian communicators to relate to people at a point of readiness. Out of private turmoil in our troubled society may come appreciation for Augustine's prayerful perspective: "Thou hast made us for thyself and our hearts are restless 'till they find their rest in thee."

Modern media have the capability of conveying the centrality of Christian faith in authentic, personal terms. The Roman Catholic theologian, Walter Ong, is concerned that we are inundated by instantaneous electronic information and "swept along without typographical man's opportunity to check back and criticize." He adds, however, "Still we have an infinitely richer store of images and impressions available to us than did book-and-print man." He claims that in depersonalizing nature, science has intensified the personal significance of man. He looks to the new communication technologies to move us toward a "new realization of the personal" and thus toward a new opportunity for "Christian living."

Practitioners in all media try to express the personal factor. When William Broyles Jr. became *Newsweek's* fifth editor-in-chief in 10 years, he was asked how he intended to change the periodical and replied, "The trick is not to go away from the news, but to give it a human dimension."

Robert Merrick, producer of many Broadway successes, when asked what makes a hit show, answered, "Something to make the audience laugh, cry, think, or a combination of these."

Actor-writer-director Alan Alda, commenting on "M*A*S*H" viewers thanking producers for progra both laughter and tears, said, "That's the way life is while you wonder how you'll get through the next 10 ....utes." The personal dimension is a much better explanation of audience involvement than McLuhan's hot-cold classification of media.

The personal is best expressed in dramatic terms, whether in print, stage, film, or broadcasting. Christian drama, for the most part, has made little impression on our generation. Between Cecil B. DeMille's sensationalized extravaganzas and church basement plays there have been sporadic but largely ineffectual attempts to revive the spirit of the medieval mystery and miracle plays which were the mass media of that age.

Does the gospel lend itself to dramatization? Or does any such attempt end in poor art? British writer Dorothy Sayers saw poor theology as the culprit. She wrote: "A loose and sentimental theology begets loose and sentimental art forms; an illogical theology lands one in illogical solutions; an ill-balanced theology issues in false emphasis and absurdity. Conversely, there is no more searching test of a theology than to submit it to dramatic handling."

The modern church has had little success in employing first-rate writers with a comprehensive understanding of the Christian faith. So our productions either avoid distinctively Christian themes or treat them in a stilted, unconvincing manner. Charles M. Schulz has demonstrated through Charlie Brown that it is possible in cartoons and films to express explicit Christian views with integrity. Meanwhile artists with no acknowledged Christian commitment recognize enough gut-level drama in our tradition to create such productions as *Jesus Christ Superstar* and *Godspell*.

Even commercial broadcasting, usually in connection with holidays, airs programs with more substance than many of our own. Several years ago "The White Shadow" featured an encounter of a basketball coach with a nun which concluded with powerful, explicitly Christian symbolism. CBS also carried a two-hour commercial special, based simply but eloquently on a church choir in the process of rehearsing the *Messiah*. In the three-hour special

"The Scarlet and the Black" CBS presented a moving account of the story of Msgr. Hugh O'Flaherty, who saved thousands of POWs from the Gestapo in Rome. Weaknesses of the bureaucratic institutional church were exposed, but the total commitment and compassion of O'Flaherty were featured against a background of Roman Catholic symbolism.

Activation in process

Even when authentically Christian programs are broadcast, nothing may happen unless their production and distribution have been planned as part of a process. The same medium-message stimulates widely different responses in different contexts. For most productive communication, interaction among participants is vital. This can be illustrated in a media effort to deal with loneliness.

A great many people in modern society are troubled by loneliness: the retired and elderly, middle-aged singles, even unpopular teenagers. The Christian church should have something to offer lonely people: the assurance that they are worth something and the support of caring companions. To say this on the air, however, is not enough. It is easy to catch attention by portraying loneliness dramatically, but more is needed. One denomination made short films available for broadcast placement by local groups who could attach their telephone numbers and invite lonely persons to make contact. When agencies took this seriously and were prepared to welcome inquiries into a continuing relationship, this was a fully developed communication process. Even a spot announcement can have value if it initiates personal contact. But this is not likely to happen if the message and process are generalized, as in ecumenical attempts: "Go to the church of your choice next Sunday."

An invitation more likely to be productive is the kind offered by a recovering alcoholic: "I spent 11 years living with an alcoholic. The alcoholic was me. The toughest phone call you will ever make is the one that may save your life. Call now." A phone number follows.

The message of the Christian faith expressed in the living color of modern media may prepare a person to respond, provided a channel for that response is immediately available. The Roman Catholic scholar Robert A. White has said, "The communicable moments when the individual and/or group are open to a crystallization of meaning and to the grace of faith are sporadic, spontaneous, and unpredictable. . . . They are likely to be moments of life-crisis, when there is a necessity of discovering some meaning." He believes, along with many religious educators, that these deeply-felt experiences are most likely to occur in a small-group context. Christian broadcasts need the kind of activation and interaction possible only in groups.

This being the case, why should our broadcasts have distinctively Christian features? Why not count on the follow-up groups to uncover the deeper implications of the faith?

Coping with a Cop-out ‖7

If media only set in motion a process to be completed in the community of believers, it would seem that church groups could be counted on to contribute whatever is explicitly Christian, allowing religious broadcasts to confine themselves to the raising of questions, arousing curiosity, identifying problems. This, however, is only a half-truth which can become a cop-out, an excuse for taking the easy route to program development.

Not all listener-viewers will come in contact with groups intending to supplement the broadcasts, leaving a serious leak in the open-ended process. Some groups themselves will not be perceptive enough to make the intended contributions and will be dependent on the broadcasts to do more than stimulate the discussion. And, finally, if all that is required is the portrayal of reality for the sake of group reflection, there is little need to invest members' contributions in such productions. Even distortions of life, as seen in soap operas and situation comedies, will serve this purpose. For these, commercial networks and films, plus PBS, with their much greater financial resources, can do a better job than churches. It is a cop-out for churches to settle for easily produced, but mediocre presentations on themes explored more creatively by others. To stay out of the media entirely, however, is a different form of cop-out. Affluent American Christians ought to be able to provide resources for production of at least a few programs sufficiently distinctive to justify the investment.

Producing programs to accomplish a clearly defined purpose requires more planning than most religious organizations are willing to undertake. In a congregation someone—perhaps an advertising agent—may have an idea for a favorite program or spot and enough money is located somehow for production costs and airtime. No one has stated the specific purpose, except to get attention for that congregation. There is no plan for continuing contact with listener-viewers and no means of discovering whether or not anyone has been affected by the broadcasts. The money is spent, nothing happens, and years must pass before new decision makers are ready to consider a new proposal.

Instead, a congregation, denomination, or ecumenical agency should consider media within the framework of overall purposes. What are our tasks and how, if at all, can the electronic media contribute to their fulfillment? With whom are we trying to engage in communication? What, exactly, are we hoping to accomplish? What medium and format are most appropriate for our purposes? What provision is made for exchange with listener-viewers? Is it possible to provide for input by telephone or interactive cable? How can contact be maintained after the presentation?

Even this is not enough. In divided Protestantism it is important to consider what other churches are doing. We may think we want to present a storytelling program for children, but if two other agencies are already doing that, perhaps we should study other options. Ideally all Christians, including Roman Catholics, would operate on a united front: the radio-TV audience doesn't make fine theological distinctions. In reality, unfortunately, denominations are often more concerned about their own recognition than oneness in Christ.

There are so many different formats for religious broadcasts that all possibilities should be considered before adopting one. A review of the most familiar types may help to correct some ingrained misunderstandings.

Experts usually write off *worship* and *devotional* broadcasts as useless. One broadcasting handbook for churches warns, "About broadcasting worship services, don't do it!" This is what I call the UFO (Uninformed Fly Over) attitude found in New York and Los Angeles. Too many communication executives have lost touch with people living west of the Hudson River and east of Anaheim. Some broadcast services, especially locally originated ones, serve substantial numbers of people—many more than are attracted to the programs distributed by the National Council of Churches, producers of the handbook. Current offerings in a particular locality should be considered before a decision is made as to whether or not to insert a worship or devotional program in the schedule.

Evidence from abroad reveals something about this type of program. In Germany and Scandinavia most people have a Christian tradition, but church attendance is notoriously infrequent. Yet in parts of those countries daily and Sunday morning radio devotionals attract a larger number of listeners than any other program. In this way the lukewarm and inactives maintain at least a bit of contact with the church. They are reminded of their heritage and of the connection between faith and daily life. In some cases they resume full participation in parish activities.

Talk programs of any length beyond 30 seconds are also dismissed by media specialists without taking into account who is talking about what. "Talking heads" are not all boring. John Bennett, former president of Union Theological Seminary in New York City, once said to his colleague Wilhelm Pauck, "You could not be uninteresting if you tried." When Henry Fonda toured with the one-actor play *Clarence Darrow*, he received a letter from a young boy saying, "My parents took me to see your play and I thought I would be bored. Boy, was I wrong!"

Leo Buscaglia, University of Southern California professor of education, embodies his own animation in TV talks delivered to large and loyal audiences on PBS. The late Francis Schaeffer, popular evangelical author, toured the country attracting crowds willing to pay substantial sums to hear him lecture hour after hour.

These are exceptions, but exceptions which demonstrate the fallacy of dismissing any possible format without taking other factors into consideration.

Interviews, with their give-and-take, have advantages over straight talk programs. Attentive interviewers can pose questions that listener-viewers would like to ask. One of the strengths of the "700 Club" and "PTL Club" is their use of interviews stimulating the contagion of personal conviction.

Interviews can probe depths. The American Broadcasting Company's Barbara Walters, interviewing the "Hill Street Blues" star Daniel J. Travanti, led him into recalling his experience as an alcoholic and asked what changed his life. He answered, "Grace, the unmerited kindness of God." Mike Wallace of CBS pressed former presidential aide Charles Colson when, in an interview, he refused to make a moral judgment on Watergate. Wallace probed, "You say you are a new man in Jesus Christ. Yet it seems as though your prior faith takes precedence over your new faith." Colson describes his reaction in his book *Born Again*: "I made no effort to wipe my face dry as Wallace wound up the interview. . . . The painful dilemma of how to live in two worlds had confronted me again, this time in living color on national TV."

Denominations could do worse than invest in travel money to place spokespersons on popular talk shows in different markets. These are actually interviews, often with live audiences or open phone lines inviting participation.

Phil Donahue, one of the best-known conductors of such programs, calls the talk show "the ultimate colloquium of today's video-oriented, high-tech world. It's town crier and it's lamp lighters." Richard Mincer, Donahue's executive producer, says, "Talk shows are among the most influential forces in our culture today." He cites the facts that millions of people tune to the more than 4000 interview programs broadcast daily in the U.S. and Canada. He estimates that a minimum of 1.7 million guest bookings occur during a year.

Allowing for the natural enthusiasm of performer and producer, this type of program does offer one of the better opportunities for participation in mainstream media. Not all guests need be celebrities. Writing a book or even holding a strong opinion may qualify for a guest spot, especially in smaller markets. Initiative must be taken, however, by the prospective guests or someone acting on their behalf. This is where denominational communication offices could invest more time and energy. It is said, "The meek may inherit the earth but they don't get booked on talk shows."

Christians who do not wish to be guests may still contribute to these programs by attending or telephoning. Volunteers could be enlisted to monitor certain programs with the expressed purpose of providing significant input. Recently while driving I heard a talk show guest make the outrageous claim that religious congregations contributing to the relief of hunger in Ethiopia were thereby supporting a repressive government and undermining democracy. The program ended before I could get to a telephone and correct this impression, planted by someone who has probably never been in Ethiopia. We who are in close touch with Christians there know that our relief and development efforts are helping the survival of persons who resist oppression and hold out the only hope for eventual liberty and justice in the land. Each day there are undoubtedly opportunities for corrective input into the public deliberative process by participating in talk shows.

Music offers program possibilities, either alone or in combination with other elements. One subtle danger must be recognized: a program of music has the advantage in station placement of appealing to program executives by appearing to be inoffensive, but this is insufficient reason for an investment of time, money, and energy.

It is possible, of course, to intersperse music with meaningful dialog. One widely distributed radio program for young people, "SCAN," features interesting interviews dealing head-on with current concerns. There are only periodic references to distinctive insights from Christian faith, but the producers intend to suggest that, since the broadcasts are a denominational "gift of love," listeners might find in the Christian community a source of help, learning, and strength. In theory, at least, this anticipates an interactive communication process.

Variety or *magazine style* programs, combining monologues, interviews, music, and feature segments, have been recognized as offering special opportunities to utilize the personal dimension of electronic media.

The "700 Club" format allows for reference to such things as exercise, gardening, nutrition, time and money management, and film reviews. There can be input from experts on topics clearly related to Christian stewardship of health, time, and possessions.

Three mainline denominations, United Presbyterians, Episcopalians, and Disciples of Christ, have been cooperating in the distribution by satellite and cable of a magazine program, "One in the Spirit." It serves principally to demonstrate the scope and vitality of work being undertaken by the participating churches.

Christian identification in the *news* is often limited to the extremes of sensationalism and the commonplace: the Sunday school teacher convicted of sexually exploiting children, or meeting times and resolutions. Church news broadcasts have some appeal, primarily for ecclesiastical professionals.

At the time of this writing an attempt is being made to develop and place a national religious news program on the order of "Washington Week in Review." A different approach would be to air discussions of current issues in which Christians, especially laypersons, would disagree while maintaining a loving relationship. This might help to convey the idea that the church is neither a monolithic entity nor a collection of uncompromising brawlers.

Through Ecumedia News Service there is an attempt to feed more important items into public news channels. The church should be having more input into the making of international policy because we are a global agency with knowledgeable contacts in most countries. Our Christian colleagues abroad often know more about social, economic, and political conditions in their countries than employees of embassies, news-gathering agencies, or transnational corporations. Lutheran leaders knew, for example, that Muzorewa was not the choice of the people to head the new government in Zimbabwe. Meanwhile U.S. government representatives, visiting primarily in cities, gave a different report to President Carter.

Church involvement in places like Nicaragua and El Salvador yields information often at variance with government and commercial media sources. We should be doing more to share our knowledge and analyses with opinion molders and decision makers. A visit to Latin America by 12 bishops of the American Lutheran Church did receive considerable coverage in the news media because their conclusions challenged national policy toward that region.

Documentaries, featuring news items, interviews, and commentary, offer possibilities for dealing with complex issues in an attention-holding manner. Docu-dramas are another variation.

One such program, titled "Don't Ask Me, Ask God," was promoted by publishing the names of such participants as Steve Allen, Jayne Meadows, Vincent Price, Ben Vereen, and Ned Beatty, without identifying Pat Robertson as the central figure. The broadcast dealt with provocative questions identified in a Gallup survey as troubling people: What does the future hold for me and my family? Why must the human race experience suffering? Why is there evil in the world today? Will there ever be world peace? Is there life after death? Robertson's answers were undoubtedly less than satisfying to many non-Christians and Christians as well, but he demonstrated a willingness to employ the media without diluting the message; contact with viewers was also invited through telephone and correspondence.

World Vision also occasionally syndicates TV specials which raise money for starving people abroad. Through interviews and dramatic vignettes they convey the apalling reality of hunger and they do not conceal the fact that they are concerned about more than physical welfare. So far mainline churches have not attempted anything on this scale.

Story and *drama* offer the strongest potential for both media and message. Theologian Robert P. Roth claims that story conveys reality better than history, philosophy, or the social sciences. He says, "When theology fails to acknowledge the story aspect of reality, it produces only tedious and prolix dissertations on Law and Gospel." The distinctive feature of Christian faith can be communicated most convincingly through lives of believers. Sociologist Robert Coles tells about Ruby Bridges, a black child involved in the early integration tensions in the South. Threatened by all sorts of dangers and taunted by fellow students, her

serene survival was a mystery to psychologists studying the phenomenon. Ruby simply explained, "At home we pray for all of
them."

"NBC Monday Night at the Movies" presented a drama,
"Choices of the Heart," that dealt with the essence of Christian
faith. It was the story of Jean Donovan, the 27-year-old American
who gave up her family, her fiance, and ultimately her life, to
be a Catholic lay missionary in wartorn El Salvador. She was
portrayed first as a carefree college student, not particularly
pious. In fact, when she first began work in El Salvador she was
challenged: "You don't want to be a nun; you disagree with much
that the church teaches. Why do you want to be a missionary;
why not the Peace Corps?"

She answered, "Because I want to bring more than food and
shoes and blankets. I want to help them come nearer to Him;
I'd like to come nearer myself and I believe this is the way I can
do it." In this case a commercial production wove message and
medium with an integrity to which most religious producers can
only aspire. Dilemmas over official and revolutionary violence
were not evaded, and even liberation theology was featured in
Archbishop Romero's words, "to walk with the poor may mean
to suffer as the poor, to suffer and die."

The only two TV programs produced by mainline churches to
appear in the top 10 religious audience figures of one rating service are "Davey and Goliath," children's puppet stories under
Lutheran auspices, and the Roman Catholic "Insight," short dramas featuring name actors. In North Dakota, "Lutherans of the
Prairie," featuring stories of individuals and congregations, has
enjoyed wide acceptance.

Full-fledged drama is too expensive for most religious organizations to undertake and credible scripts are scarce, but other
forms of presenting stories offer alternatives.

Imported ideas

In the U.S. we could profit by studying the media efforts of
churches elsewhere in the world. In the Netherlands, Germany,
and Scandinavia religious broadcasting is more than a vestigial

appendage. With the new availability of local radio stations and cable TV in parts of Europe there is increased involvement of churches.

Occasional programs from overseas might be of sufficient interest to be aired in this country. African church leaders are especially vocal in claiming that there is a spiritual lethargy in the West which could be addressed by committed Christians from elsewhere. Programs from abroad might help to strengthen our sense of a global community of believers.

Internal values

Whatever the format, the new media, especially cable, offer opportunity for increased placement of programs. Inexpensive videotape equipment can expedite production and extend off-the-air distribution. Commercial producers have discovered that young people, especially, have favorite videotapes which they play over and over, enjoying the repetition of familiar scenes. It would be quite an accomplishment if the church could produce cassettes with such an appeal.

There is already available a video game cartridge which fascinates preteens and young teens. They cluster around a video monitor taking turns pushing a joy stick and amassing points. But they are not evading monsters or launching missiles; they're rescuing an unknown friend from a maze of poverty. The purpose of the game, called Eachone Reachone, is to create an awareness of world hunger and what can be done about it and to teach global awareness. Designed for the volunteer organization Save the Children and Columbia Teachers College, the game has been shared with Lutheran World Relief. That agency expects to create other games for similar purposes.

The influence of many religious programs will be primarily internal—within the Christian community. This is not all bad. Surveys indicate a disappointing lack of knowledge among Christians about our faith. Advertisers of everything from Pepsi-Cola to Buicks are not only intent on winning new customers, but on holding present ones. Inner strength is important for being "builded together for a habitation of God" (Eph. 2:22 KJV), and also is essential for outreach. Even in simple terms of publicity, internal communication is the place to begin. Communication consultant Russ Reid says, "Now the first thing you have to do in publicizing something about your church to your community is to publicize what is going on in your church to your own people. You need to create a sense of God at work in your own church—to your own people—before you worry about talking to the community."

This does not mean, as we shall see, that modern media are useless in evangelism.

Prospects for 8
Evangelism

"We never have believed that through television we could truly evangelize or communicate the core of the gospel," declared William F. Fore in one of his annual reports to the Board of Managers of the National Council's Communication Commission. Yet later in the same meeting the staff distributed quotations from audience mail, including the following:

> I am not an overly religious man, and I seldom watch television. But somehow, and I don't believe by accident, I ended up watching the special Cotton Patch run today at 1:00 P.M. I cannot tell you how meaningful that was for me; I stopped and took a good look at my own life, and the way I approach it. It changed me.

Fore is one of the most knowledgeable scholars of Christian communication in the world, but even he does not like to be confused by facts. The party line among religious communication specialists has been that broadcasting is an inappropriate medium through which to undertake evangelism; contradictory evidence is simply disregarded. In Japan after World War II one religious radio series was so influential that 26 pastors now active in the Japanese Lutheran Churches came to faith through that program. It was the Japan Lutheran Hour, featuring dramas of Christian life. More recently congregations have been founded in Brazil by Lutheran Hour listeners in that country. In Ethiopia and Tanzania so many persons were brought to the Christian faith through radio that there was a serious scarcity of trained leaders to serve new congregations.

All play and no work

The fact that broadcasting in this country does operate under different conditions offers a convenient excuse for not undertaking an admittedly difficult task. There is even a philosophical base for such an escape in William Stephenson's play theory: life is divided into work and play, with radio and TV functioning only in the area of play. Communication scholar Wilbur Schramm claims that the trouble with such single-factor theories is that they explain so much that they explain nothing. He says, "By choosing to detour attention from the information function, Stephenson ignores the quality that chiefly distinguishes communication from other behavior. . . . Explaining the function of communication in terms of work and play runs into the fact that these categories blur into one another." Many of us have been fortunate enough to work at tasks that were at least as enjoyable as play. Is it work or play to make a discovery in research? Indulging in love for truth and beauty may be a mixture of work and play. As Schramm says of Stephenson's concepts, "The really interesting distinctions may be within rather than between such categories."

Instead of dismissing the electronic media as instruments only of play and the frivolous, they should be considered for other possibilities. Are they capable of directing attention and interest to more serious matters?

It is mainline religious broadcasters, for the most part, who dismiss employment of electronic media in evangelism. Evangelicals and independents claim to be busily engaged in outreach although, as we have observed, the extent of their reach is open to question. A program attempting to stimulate the outsider instead of gratifying the faithful is unlikely to raise large amounts of money. Dave Breese of "Back to the Bible" ministry explained why their separate evangelistic effort, "Pause for Good News," could not be expected to become self-supporting: "The potential for the response of faith is great, but the mail response is minimal.

listener will rarely write and almost never make a
n." For this obvious reason broadcasters who are in-
                of denominations but dependent on audience contri-
butions end up appealing to the faithful despite their intentions
to evangelize.

Apart from the media, mainline denominations talk a great deal
about evangelism but little seems to happen. To some extent this
uncovers an embarrassment over accusations of proselytism, or
forcing one's convictions on others. Instead of the cowboy (rope
and brand) image, mainliners prefer to be regarded as shepherds
(feed and lead). But shepherds prod the lethargic and search for
the missing. There is a difference between trying to force an
unwanted conviction on someone and offering to share a treasure.
Modern environmentalists have a deep sense of wanting to preserve and share the tremendous physical resources of this planet.
Christians are similarly concerned with preserving and sharing
the resources of the gospel.

Work as witness?

Not all rejection of electronic evangelism is based on a re-
luctance to attempt anything serious through the media. As we
have noted, some mainline religious broadcasts do reflect a strong
sense of social responsibility. How does this relate to evangelism?
The question reflects an old theological debate.

From the experience of evangelism emerge believers who act
in love. Their work may then be evident to others and contribute
to a new stage of evangelism. Work of Christians, such as social
action, may thus become an element in witness. Is the work itself
sufficient witness? Can it be identified with evangelism, or is
more involved? Theologian Martin Marty says:

For me, to evangelize means to meet people in situations
where the Gospel of Jesus Christ is given the opportunity
to change individuals and groups and to bring them toward
wholeness. Evangelism, in other words, is to "save" them
and to situate them in the context of Christian community
so that their lives will be enhanced. Then they can face

together those questions of values, meanings and service that have eternal dimensions.

Note that, for Marty, dealing with questions of value and meaning becomes possible *after* people have been changed and situated within a community of believers.

Communication specialists might accept Marty's definition and argue that the modern media are inappropriate instruments for evangelism because (1) they reach so few "outsiders" and (2) they present so partial an element of the gospel.

Outsiders and insiders

It is a mistake to draw a sharp line between religious insiders and outsiders in the United States. Most Americans have something of a biblical heritage, no matter how faint. Gallup surveys indicate that large majorities believe in the divinity of Christ, the uniqueness of the Bible, and the importance of prayer.

Instead of a dividing line between believers and unbelievers, there is a long spectrum of differing attitudes. At one end are the radical fundamentalists who subscribe to particular words and codes, and are suspicious of all who disagree with them. At the other extreme are militant atheists, adamant in their opinion of religion as a vestigal form of primitive superstition.

Along the broad band in the middle, comprising at least two-thirds of the population, are persons with varying degrees of connection with organized religion, but with an openness toward something of potential significance for their lives. In Morris West's novel, *Clowns of God*, the atheistic professor of psychiatry, Anneliese Meissner, says, "I read the omens in every newspaper. I hear the distant drums and the mad trumpets. . . . I think we'll have our Armageddon. I dream about it every night—and I wish I could find a faith to comfort me in the dark."

Statistics from the Annenberg-Gallup study of religious television yielded the usual evidence that few Americans claim to have no denominational ties but more than one-third of the unaffiliated were identified as viewers of religious TV. The study also revealed that, among viewers, more than one-third attend church less than once a week; most of that one-third, in fact, attend less than once a month. The fact that no religious program has an audience comparable to the top entertainment shows, and that only a minority of those listener-viewers are unchurched, should not be misinterpreted. Broadcasting is such a pervasive medium that crumbs that fall from the networks' tables may represent far more outsiders than are reached by any other method undertaken by the church. The typical congregation attracts very few, if any, unchurched to regular worship services. Even a few hundred media contacts present an opportunity.

But isn't communication with outsiders altogether different from internal preaching and teaching? Not necessarily. Preachers who assume that their captive audience is listening and learning are under an illusion. The typical occupant of a mainline pew is not necessarily more receptive to a sermon than a casual listener-viewer to a broadcast. It is true that the church member has chosen to be present, but habit or custom may have affected this. It is possible to switch mental channels in church. On the other hand, the person who stays tuned to a religious broadcast may do so because of a pressing need to which the program seems to be addressing itself.

Southern Baptists used an advertising campaign to explore the possibility that some unchurched people are receptive to an explicitly religious invitation. Ads were run in the *National Enquirer*, a weekly tabloid known for its sensationalism. The Baptists were hoping to reach outsiders and reasoned that readers of the *Enquirer* were not likely to be actively involved in the church. Placed in the personals column, the copy read, "Bible Study magazine, easy to see and understand. Beautiful and free. Southern Baptist Convention, Nashville, Tennessee." Hundreds of replies were received.

Both insiders and outsiders, members and nonmembers, converted and unconverted, have fears and hopes, needs and desires, joys and sorrows to which the gospel speaks with explosive power. The only question is whether the messenger can provide the igniting spark to release that power. Communication and community have a common root. When we discover what we have in common with God's other loved ones we are able to communicate and realize that we are part of a community. We are no longer foreigners or strangers; we "are now fellow citizens with God's people and members of the family of God" (Eph. 2:19 TEV). This can be welcome news.

How much is enough?

Electronic media are also regarded as doubtful instruments for evangelism because any religious message conveyed through them is likely to be only partial, a small fragment of the whole gospel. As already observed, however, nearly all presentations, except for lengthy theological treatises, are partial. An attempt to say everything is likely to communicate nothing, whether on TV or from the pulpit. The German theologian Helmut Thielicke says, "He who attempts to bring the whole schema of Trinity, creation, redemption and eschatology into his sermon cannot help but produce a pale and diluted effect."

How much must be attempted to make the effort worthwhile? It is not a question of quantity but centrality. Thielicke says, "One must have the courage to make one central point and therefore be content to be incomplete. We must let the rabbits go today . . . because today we are hunting stags." If somehow we can convey the essential feature of the Scriptures—God's unconditional love for all creation, revealed in Christ—we need not be overly concerned with what we are omitting.

It is tempting, however, to settle for rabbits because they are so much more numerous and so much easier to pursue. We focus on questions people are already asking, without probing into the broken divine-human relationship underneath the questions. We duplicate what can be done as well or better by PBS, social service and mental agencies, Alcoholics Anonymous, the Red Cross, and the American Civil Liberties Union. It is not surprising that little is accomplished in terms of evangelism.

Ineffectual use of the media by mainline churches is due partly to bureaucratic separation of responsibilities. Evangelism departments often have little knowledge of media, and media specialists have little interest in evangelism. Communication executives characteristically develop "shows" which satisfy their sense of creativity and have some opportunity for being aired.

Priorities of communication offices are not always correlated with denominational emphases.

Congregations are urged to apply the element of process to broadcasts distributed by national offices. Seldom, however, are congregations involved in the earliest stages of program planning.

Since evangelism is most likely to occur in the congregational setting, there should be input at the outset from members actually engaged in outreach. Congregations should identify their particular prospects for outreach, allowing the creation of programs related to those prospects.

Members must be prepared not only to encourage listening-viewing by unchurched friends, but to converse with them afterwards. This will require some familiarity with the programs and consideration of how best to engage in discussion about them.

There should also be continuing examination of the process to determine its effectiveness. A pilot study with a few programs prior to distribution of an entire series can make possible helpful changes—or drastic revision of the entire project.

Congregational cultivation

Under these conditions the partial nature of most electronic communication can be taken into account. Conversing by telephone is not the most satisfying element of courtship, but in the facet of separation it can be deeply influential. Radio and TV can introduce potentially crucial and decisive elements into the evangelism process, but there is still need for more than one-way transmission. Luther could say, "While I sit here drinking my pot of Wittenberg beer, the gospel runs its course," but he had set in motion an extensive educational effort.

Religious broadcasters often receive letters from people who have been deeply moved by particular programs. This is especially true if mail is encouraged by offering to send transcripts of the programs or other relevant material.

One listener to "SCAN," the music and interview program for young people, wrote:

You do good work; that's saying a lot, coming from me. I used to go to church every Sunday but slid away from the tradition and routine I was taught. I'm not knocking religion—just hypocritical churches which don't teach kids the basic grassroots stuff they need to grow on.

I got more out of hearing one of your broadcasts than a month of Sundays could have enlightened me. It said, "You realize, of course, that Jesus Christ said that people who take him seriously are going to have three things happen to them: they are going to know joy and happiness, people are going to think they are crazy, and they are going to get into trouble."

I'll be a fool for Christ because I care.

For this person, involvement in a caring community is essential, but arranging for the contact is a precarious venture. He or she may be turned off by some congregations, but can find what is needed in others.

The scriptural story of the sower applies to this predicament. Some seeds fall on a path where they are stepped on or eaten by birds; the momentary inspiration of a broadcast may be obliterated by succeeding hours of escapist programming. Some fall among thorns and weeds which grow up and choke them; the searching listener-viewer will be the object of all sorts of seductive appeals from competing faiths, religious and otherwise. Some fall on rocky ground where, lacking moisture, they dry up and die; simply wandering into the nearest church on the next Sunday may snuff out the flickering flame kindled by a broadcast. Landing in good soil, some seeds grow and produce grain; there are many lively congregations where faith will be enriched, but connecting a troubled or perplexed inquirer with the right one is no easy task.

Completing the communication circle, so important to evangelism, is especially difficult with nationally distributed series which cannot possibly take into account the distinctive characteristics of various congregations. Locally originated programs have a distinct advantage in that they can stress existing features of their ministry and avoid false claims.

Congregations which make serious, thoughtful attempts to integrate the public media in their evangelism efforts are sometimes surprised and sobered by the results. I remember consulting once with Christians in Tehran concerning the possibility of producing shortwave broadcasts to be beamed from Ethiopia into Iran. At first they were excited by the prospect of actually hearing Christian programs in their own language, Farsi, coming through the air into their homes. But then, when it was realized that non-Christians might also hear the same broadcasts and come inquiring about the faith, there were hesitations; encouraging Muslims to consider Christianity involved great dangers.

The situation in this country is different, but we also need to be prepared to respond actively to indications of interest. When a Minnesota congregation began presenting an hour-long interview and variety program on a religious TV station at 11 A.M. on Sunday, it was soon discovered that viewers included outsiders, some of whom wished to become members. Children in foster homes and halfway houses were found to be watching. Parents who only sent their children to church school used this opportunity to monitor what was going on. Fortunately, that congregation was accustomed to welcoming newcomers and enlisting them in ministry. Residents of a state prison were also encouraged to watch the programs, and when these men became eligible for release, members of the congregation assisted them in relocation and rehabilitation. Going public through the mass media can be a reminder of the many dimensions of evangelism.

This experience, repeated in other localities, is a clear refutation of the claim that TV cannot be employed in evangelism. A religious station may not provide the best channel for reaching the unchurched and Sunday morning is often dismissed as the location of the religious ghetto. In fact, however, Sunday morning has the advantage of offering a subconscious appeal to people who once observed this as a time for worship and who might give attention then to something which they would tune out immediately at other times of the week. And the audience for a religious station will probably include more lukewarm outsiders than are likely to make the trip to a sanctuary on a given Sunday.

The only congregations willing to make an investment of, say $100,000 annually, in so risky an evangelism effort, are likely to be fundamentalistic or charismatic, giving a narrow impression

of the Christian faith to persons having had little re
with the church. While some searching inactives will
others will be repelled.

Some mainline congregations have found that raising money
for such a project is not out of the question; memorials and other
special gifts are often subscribed for this purpose. It is also possible for several congregations to share both cost and responsibility for a continuing series, but this dilutes identification of the
program with a single, regularly gathered community.

World mission

Since radio and TV do cross boundaries, both cultural and
geographical, they appear to offer possibilities for global evangelism. Sixty missionary radio stations employing 128 transmit-
ters are broadcasting in more than 100 languages.

The familiar exhortation, "Go therefore and make disciples of
all nations" (Matt. 28:19), sounds like an authorization to broadcast, but international conditions are different from the time when
Paul, who was both a Jew and a Roman citizen, could travel
around the known world without being a foreigner. Sending signals into another nation today is both an opportunity and a hazard.
Unwisely undertaken, it can handicap the Christian residents in
the receiving land.

In nearly every country in the modern world there is an in-
digenous church whose members are best prepared to communicate the gospel to their fellow citizens. Where Christians are
a small minority, they are often suspected of holding to an alien
faith. For the sake of their ministry it is important that procla-
mation of the gospel not take a form which can be interpreted as
cultural imperialism. This is a special danger where East-West
tensions prevail.

Roman Catholics have known that the church was alive in Po-
land; Lutherans have been encouraged by the persistence of the
faith in East Germany. Even in the Soviet Union and China it
has become evident that religion has not disappeared as previously predicted. It is possible, of course, that international shortwave broadcasts have helped to spread the seeds of faith across

the barren steppes of the east, but it is also possible for interfering westerners to trample down tender plants before they can bloom.

According to one study, Soviet Christians are sharply critical of the many hours of Christian broadcasting beamed by shortwave radio to the USSR each week. Believers there complain that "platitudes and things they already know" fill much of the broadcasting time. One Soviet Christian commented, "We don't need to have atheist teaching disproved all the time and to be told that God does exist. This is elementary." Another complained that the "music . . . is an insult to listeners" and the preaching style is "far too emotional, too excited for Russians."

It is usually a mistake for broadcasts intended for the United States simply to be translated and beamed to other nations. It is far better, when possible, to assist churches from within a country to prepare programs for broadcast to that land. Ideally, these can be placed on local stations. In some African countries churches have access to broadcast time but need help with production costs. In Arequipa, Peru, 70% of the people listen to a local program of the Norwegian Lutheran Mission. In southern Brazil the Lutheran Church owns and operates a small network of radio stations.

When internal placement is impossible, recorded tapes can be broadcast from distant stations. Shortwave is the main information medium in many parts of the world, and transistor sets are common possessions of even the poor. Bible correspondence courses and other study materials supplement broadcasts. This was the procedure for Radio Voice of the Gospel when it was transmitting from Ethiopia. Tapes were supplied from studios in different parts of Africa, the Middle East, and India, produced by the churches of those countries to be beamed by directional antennae back to their fellow citizens. One such ministry developed widespread interest in Christianity among the wandering Fulani tribes in northern Africa.

The Middle East Lutheran Ministry, broadcasting from Monaco, Cyprus, and Beirut, stimulates correspondence from young people in North Africa, 70% of whom are non-Christians.

In rare cases, such as in Ethiopia and China today, there is governmental opposition to such transnational broadcasting.

Then the global church faces a difficult policy decision. Most laypersons probably welcome Christian programs from abroad, especially since they are not available locally. Government opposition, however, can result in restrictions on internal church activity and national church leaders must at least appear publicly to discourage such attempts. Any such concession to political pressures seems to contradict the universal nature of the Christian church, but may be the lesser of two evils if the local church itself is not to be prohibited from carrying on its work of education and evangelism. In Ethiopia an extensive cassette project serves as something of a replacement for the previous broadcasts.

In many countries of the Third World cassettes offer a major opportunity for outreach. The Iranian population was conditioned for revolution against the Shah by distribution of cassettes. Even video cassettes are multiplying in unexpected places. India has only one car or telephone for every 100 in the United States, but one VCR for every 15 in America. Most Third World churches are eager to take advantage of such obvious opportunities, but need help from their more affluent brothers and sisters in the North and West.

Acknowledging opportunities for electronic evangelism should not sweep us into regarding modern media as a panacea for the world's ills. The influence of broadcasts produced by churches is unlikely to make a substantial ripple in the commercial tide pounding the shores of our electronic age. Christians should pursue more creative attempts to be seen and heard. Above all, we must learn to respond to the emerging media which occupy so much of people's lives, and to raise a voice in the wilderness regarding a system more concerned with profits than values. In the final chapters we will focus on these tasks.

PART THREE

The Road Ahead

Needed: A New Audience ‖9

Members of a Christian sect in Lapland waged a campaign to save people from going to hell by smashing their television sets. In one community the sect even condemned washing machines with windows because they allow men to view women's personal garments.

We have noted that in the United States Jerry Mander has proposed doing away with television. Going to such extremes may serve to focus attention on dangers of the modern media, but the media are not going to disappear, because so many people are satisfied with them. One group of guilt-free television addicts has even formed an organization, the Couch Potatoes, advocating prolonged TV viewing. With their female auxiliary, the Couch Tomatoes, these satirists engage in marathon viewing sessions and celebrate "the recline of Western civilization."

Audience choices

More serious are the frequent incidents revealing audience preferences. When Kansas City television stations pre-empted afternoon soap operas for coverage of the shooting of Pope John Paul II, hundreds of viewers called to complain and, in some cases, threaten violence. KCMO-TV received nearly 500 angry calls and KMBC-TV logged 278 complaints, in addition to about 70 calls so abusive the switchboard operator cut them off. At

KMBC the station's front door was locked after one couple threatened to come and burn the station down.

A revealing special on Cambodia was aired in prime time by a Minneapolis TV station and attracted a respectable audience, but also drew 150 telephoned complaints before the operator wrote on the log that there were too many to count. Typical comments included: "Get that Cambodia junk off"; "If I wanted to be depressed I would have turned to something that would make me depressed"; "Tell Al Austin to take care of starving children in his own country before going to Cambodia"; and, from many, "Why isn't 'The Jeffersons' on?"

The sports pundit Howard Cosell, during an interview, asked rhetorically, "You know what the major problem with television is in this country?" As always, Cosell was not unprepared to answer his own question. "It's not television's problem. The problem is the lowness of the mass intelligent quotient. What do you do? How do you bring quality to a medium? It's a major problem!"

The quality of mass media programming in the United States is a problem, all right, and industry, while far from innocent, is not the only guilty party. Changes are needed in management and regulation, but the greatest need may be for a new audience, composed of more discriminating consumers. Cosell is wrong in diagnosing the ailment as low I.Q. Millions of intelligent people are misusing the output of the public media. Our educational system has had trouble teaching people to read; it has hardly begun the process of cultivating tastes and helping students to learn to listen carefully, to watch thoughtfully, and to respond meaningfully to multimedia communication symbols. As electronic input is multiplied by cable, satellite, computer, and VCR, the ability to discriminate increases in importance. That ability can be learned by persons within a wide range of intelligence. It is at this point that schools and churches have their primary responsibility in entering the electronic age.

Time limits

Television has been described as a drug, one which induces an "alpha" brain rhythm, relaxing us until we are uncritically receptive to whatever appears on the flickering screen. Not all programs are sedatives; some are stimulants, but both can be addictive. As with some other drugs, while use in moderation may be helpful, the possibility of addiction is a real and present danger.

Physicians have identified the "tired child syndrome" as a demonstrable result, in some children, of excessive TV viewing. In one study two pediatricians, Drs. Richard M. Narkewitz and Stanley N. Graven, examined a group of children suffering from tiredness, anorexia, headache, abdominal pain, sleep disturbance, and vomiting. All were found to be avid television viewers, watching from 3 to 6 hours per weekday and 6 to 10 hours per day on weekends. This constituted considerably more viewing than the amount reported for a random group of similar children not suffering the same symptoms. As therapy, television viewing was either stopped or strictly limited and, in some cases, mild bedtime sedatives were prescribed for short periods. Parents were urged to have their children engage in physical exercise after school and in quiet recreational activities in the evening. All of the children soon showed marked improvement and symptoms gradually disappeared. Later, however, children who again were permitted unrestricted television viewing resumed the original condition of anxiety.

The physicians concluded: "The syndrome seems to be a self-perpetuating cycle in which the anxiety interferes with sound sleep at night, leaves the child too tired to engage in outside activities and less able to withstand emotional stress the following day. This results in his spending more time watching television, getting more anxious, sleeping less well and awakening less able to do anything but watch more television. . . . The conscientious, introspective, sensitive and probably insecure children who invariably become emotionally involved in the programs appear to be most susceptible to this syndrome."

In this study it was observed that the therapy was sometimes difficult to apply because parents had trouble restricting their children's viewing. New tensions arose in the process of making necessary decisions. TV is likely to have its most harmful effects in situations where there is the least family discipline.

Parents exercise some care in employing baby-sitters, but TV is often used indiscriminately for this purpose. Before buying a home, parents also inquire about the quality of schools in the district; less consideration is given to the educational effect of a medium occupying as much of a child's time as school.

The sheer amount of time spent viewing the tube is critical not only because of the potential harm caused, but also because of the good possibilities missed. With adolescence there usually comes a drop in viewing time because other activities gain in attractiveness. Younger children are more dependent on adults to assist in making such activities available.

Children are not the only ones susceptible to addiction from overexposure to TV. All members of a family should decide in advance how much time is going to be devoted to watching the cathode ray tube. Program listings should be studied and viewing scheduled to balance with other activities. Attendance at concerts, sporting events, and theaters is usually planned in advance; TV schedules should be studied with equal care. This requires some discipline, because tickets need not be purchased in advance and it is easier to sit back and push buttons than to take more initiative in our stewardship of time.

One California physician concocted an ingenious device for limiting his own viewing time. He connected his stationary exercise bike with a generator providing the only source of electricity to his television set. One hour of vigorous pedaling was enough to operate the TV set for an equal amount of time.

Another means of taking human nature into account is the lockout button which cable companies can provide parents for restricting children's viewing. Such extreme methods are of dubious value; if families cannot agree on the distribution of time, technical deterrents are not likely to be effective.

To engage in self-examination concerning allocation of time, family members may ask themselves certain questions.

- How much time do I spend watching TV each week?
- How does this compare with the time I devote to other voluntary pursuits, such as reading, vigorous exercise, musical practice, stimulating games, etc.?

- Do I ever turn on the set without knowing what's on? (Would I go the the theater without knowing what was playing?)
- Do I ever tune out a program which is uninteresting or offensive? (If not, there is reason to question my judgment.)
- How difficult is it for me to leave the dream world of TV and return to my daily routine? (Pain relievers are helpful so long as they are not used to conceal a serious illness.)
- Can I get along without TV when I am out of range, as in camping? Or must I have my daily injection?
- Do we turn off the TV set whenever someone comes to visit? (This may be more a question of manners than of discrimination.)
- Do we watch TV during meals instead of engaging in conversation? (In exceptional cases special programs may stimulate discussion.)

Answers to these questions should help a family discover the extent to which TV is becoming an addiction instead of a planned use of time.

Not all bad

One theory in football holds that "the best defense is a good offense." Records indicate that neither one is worth much without the other. In confronting the electronic age, Christians should not only be on guard against the dangers but be alert to take advantage of opportunities. In the book *Democratic Vistas*, titled from a Walt Whitman poem, David Marc contends that Whitman's vision of a truly democratic cultural form has been realized in television. Admitting that much of TV fare is tripe, Marc warns that we make a serious mistake if we overlook television as a vast repository of cultural images and ideas.

One of the earliest research efforts in television studied effects on 6000 children, supplemented with information from 2300 parents, teachers, and school officials. In the book which emerged, *Television in the Lives of Our Children*, the three authors, Wilbur Schramm, Jack Lyle, and Edwin B. Parker, traced a progression in questioning. Instead of inquiring, "What is television doing to our children?" they suggested we should be asking ourselves,

"What are our children doing with television?" A further refinement might take the form of a statement, "What television is doing to our children depends, to a great extent, on what our children are doing with television." This conclusion is even more valid with the availability of newer, potentially interactive media.

We have noted elsewhere that modern psychologists no longer regard visual attention as primarily reactive but as actively under the control of the viewer. Christians know that we are not simply targets for electronic ballistics, but we are marvelous organisms created in the image of God. Efforts to account for the impact of electronic media should consider what viewers bring to that experience at least as much as what the media bring to viewers.

Even young people are not automatically harmed by TV exposure. One major study concluded that up to 10 hours of television viewing per week may enhance academic achievement. A research project of the California Department of Education revealed that regular viewers of "M*A*S*H" and news programs had higher achievement scores than other students. It is certainly as likely that brighter students chose to watch those programs as that they were enlightened by them, but at least they were apparently not contaminated in the process.

While it is true that children generally see television as less demanding than other media such as print, and therefore expect to expend less effort in learning from TV programs, when they are alerted to educational possibilities they discover a new outlet for their natural curiosity. One research project, using electroencephalographs ("brain wave machines"), showed patterns of greater cerebral activity in response to some instructional televised materials than for reading.

Watching together

New audiences may be created by families and peer groups watching telecasts together and talking about them. Videotape recorders facilitate this process. Programs aired at odd hours may be seen when mutually convenient.

Modern entertainment media are criticized for dealing with subjects previously regarded as taboo, but this fact presents an opportunity to families, schools, and churches. Popular programs bring into the open situations, language, standards, and patterns of action that might be difficult or awkward to introduce in traditional settings. When a neutral third party has aired specifics of a touchy issue, both young and old, authority figure and rebel, conservative and liberal, are more likely to enter into discussion. Instead of opposing the presentation of sexual themes in family viewing time, it might be wiser to schedule group attention to such programs. It would be better for young people to consider them in a family setting than simply to be exposed to them in a porn theater.

On the TV series "Different Strokes" two programs portrayed the danger from child molesters. Through a believable experience involving the young characters Arnold and Dudley with an overly friendly bicycle merchant, children were helped to recognize suspicious characteristics.

Imaginary experiences with evil can be instructive. As a medieval philosopher stated, "Experience is the worst teacher; too many die from it before they learn." The electronic media are able to involve the viewer in vicarious experiences that extend our grasp of reality and correct what might be an intellectual imbalance.

What the French philosopher Gabriel Marcel wrote about the cinema applies to the electronic media as well. He attributed to film the power of deepening and rendering more intimate "our relation to this Earth which is our habitat," and added, "To me who has always had the propensity to get tired of what I have the habit of seeing—what in reality I do not see anymore—this power . . . seems to be literally redeeming."

In our concern for concepts and doctrines Christians may similarly overlook concrete experiences and thus fail to perceive the total dimension of faith. We may relegate the spiritual to certain times and categories apparently unrelated to our daily physical, material, and emotional experiences. The gospel demands that we relate the New Testament to the newspaper, the "NBC Movie of the Week" to the drama of God's love in the person of Jesus Christ.

You ought to be in pictures

If we are to benefit from experiences in the electronic age, if we are to grow instead of stagnate, we must enter actively into the viewing process. We must put ourselves into the pictures, reacting and responding to the situations and relationships portrayed there.

After seeing a program we can reflect on our participation. *Why did I watch that program? What effect, if any, is it likely to have on me?*

There is nothing wrong with admitting that I watch some programs only to relax, but is this always my only purpose? Is relaxation the only result, or has the program had a subtle effect on me? One U.S. surgeon general, C. Everett Koop, claimed that the real issue in the debate over televised violence is, "Why on earth does anybody watch that stuff?" Do we get our kicks out of seeing brutality? What are my feelings when the hero is bashing the villain? Does this mean I regard violence as the best solution for problems? Am I a spectator who would stand aside while someone is being assaulted? My emotional reaction to dramatic presentations can be a healthy form of self-examination.

Fantasy—reality

One commonly expressed fear about the popular media is that the fantasies they portray may be confused with reality. Dr. Darold Treffert, director of a Mental Health Institute, has blamed the spiraling rate of teenage suicides on the "American fairy tale." He has observed that young people are led to believe "they'll be successful, have two cars, a swimming pool; that they'll marry, have beautiful children, and live happily ever after." When they come face to face with reality, which may include drugs, poverty, crime and unemployment, they can't take it. "For some youth," Treffert says, "the fairy tale ends in suicide, for others, in psychiatric hospitals, where half the patients are under 21."

Do children regularly confuse electronic fantasy with reality? No, according to a team of Harvard University researchers, conducting a long-term study of television's effects on the way children think and act. The researchers report that children as young as age two begin to make distinctions between TV fantasy and reality of home and parents. Although television may distort children's ideas about people and places outside their experience, it does not confuse them about the world they know. It may even stimulate them to draw lines between fantasy and reality by testing those concepts.

In one study of the Harvard project, researchers selected three children and monitored their TV viewing over three years, visiting them and observing them in their homes. One child was totally absorbed with television while another played with friends in front of the screen, treating the telecast as background noise. The third child used television as a springboard for discussion, commenting on the action and asking questions about it. The responses of this third child demonstrate that our proposed "new audience" can learn to distinguish reality from fantasy.

Children are not alone in needing to develop this ability. Soap operas are commonly accused of disrupting marriages by innoculating homebound wives with unrealistic expectations. Macho action shows cultivate male disillusionment.

There are questions to help persons of all ages distinguish between fantasy and reality. *Is the dramatic situation believable? Is there stereotyping according to age, sex, or race? Are actions of the characters clearly motivated or contrived? Is the central conflict in the plot resolved in a likely way or is it settled too easily? Could there be a more believable solution?*

Whether or not a story is divided into the traditional three acts, it usually follows the progression: (1) put the leading characters up a tree; (2) throw stones at them; and (3) bring them down from the tree. A romantic variation has boy meet girl, boy lose girl, boy find girl. Each stage of plot development invites discussion about whether this would really happen, and if so, why. Imagination can also be stimulated by speculating about different directions which the story could have taken.

People or puppets

On the lighted tube we are introduced to many different people, some heroic, some pathetic, some little more than puppets. The Jesuit scholar Father William Lynch contends that art and theology come together at the point where they both wish to say "that man is a complicated and fascinating being, whether for good or bad." He questions "whether or not the mass arts are creating a flat and neutral image of man that seldom in its sensibility touches the heights and depths of reality as it is described by Christianity."

One of the skills in acting is to pay close attention to all that is happening onstage and to react naturally to what other actors are saying and doing. As participant-observers in media productions, we should also be reacting to the characters, noticing whether they are full-dimensional people or only puppets used by writers to create a phony scene. Again, there are questions to be asked.

Is there any character too good or too strong to be believable? Anyone too bad or too weak to be human? Which character would I most like to be or know? Why? Which one would I least like to be or know?

My answers will reveal something about my ambitions, disappointments, life purpose, and hopes. The comedy writer Stanley Shapiro, explaining his insistence on opulence in his scripts, explained, "People don't want to see themselves on the screen. They don't want to see their ordinary, everyday surroundings. They want to see something better, something they can hope for. That's what I try to give them—not messages, but hope. It's like—like religion."

Whose hopes are attractive to us? When we see someone like Willie Loman in the classic *Death of a Salesman* fall apart and hear his son say, "He never knew who he was," we can compare our lives with Willie's and wonder whether we know who we are. Parents whose marriage is disintegrating may view one of various productions portraying the agony of both adults and children when a family is broken, and reconsider their options.

Our laugh track

Many situation comedies use recorded laughter in an effort to bolster response to the intended humor. Instead of allowing ourselves to be infected by this artificial contagion, we can think about our own spontaneous response. *What seems to be funniest to me? Why do I laugh? Do I ever laugh at persons because they remind me of myself?*

Much humor consists of making fun of someone else. We laugh at a person who trips over a rake because we feel superior to the clumsy oaf. Yet if the person is injured, our laughter is replaced by an attempt to be of assistance. There is a narrow line between the humor of supremacy and the solidarity of compassion. Even as we watch people making fools of themselves, we realize that we might find ourselves in the same predicament. Laughing *with* someone, or actually laughing at ourselves, can be a form a sharing.

What about far-out characters like Archie Bunker? Some people were laughing at him because he was so outrageous and others because he was airing sentiments they were secretly delighted to hear expressed. At the least, prejudices were being ventilated. In this connection the comments of a Scottish-American sociologist may stimulate our thinking. Hugh Dalziel Duncan has said, "All comedy is a form of sanctioned disrespect. . . . In laughter we are prepared to cure what we are laughing at. When laughter stops, revolt begins, and incongruity becomes an evil that cannot be tolerated in critical discussion, but must be stamped out in war and violence."

It was sad when there could be comedy at the expense of blacks but not whites, and women but not men. It is equally sad if we cannot laugh with each other at both of us. When we can share humor at our mutual foibles, genuine communication will be enhanced.

Sexuality

In the commercial battle to attract attention, sex is a powerful weapon. When television began making inroads into theatrical film audiences, motion picture producers started offering inducements not available on the home screen: pictures that dealt explicitly with nudity and sex. Since such programs had special appeal for viewers television wanted most to reach—the age group of 18 to 49—television soon stretched its standards and began showing many of the same movies, slightly edited. Then boundaries were extended for other programs as well, resulting in what *New York Times* television critic Les Brown has described as "a bizarre cycle—the motion picture industry staying ahead of television to keep its audience, and television imitating what succeeded in the movies, with the rationale that the moral values of the country were changing and that it was merely keeping up with the times." Cable and video recorders are accelerating the process. Critics try to draw distinctions between "hard-core pornography" and "erotic realism."

One response to this new wave of sexually explicit programming is to oppose its distribution, a task involving difficulties to be considered in our final chapter. Another response is the simple refusal to watch such programs. In fact, however, many otherwise excellent telecasts include portrayals of sexual relationships and activities at variance with Christian tradition. And the portrayals are not surprising to anyone familiar with contemporary lifestyles.

Society has a primary concern for the influence of such programs on children and young people. There is disagreement about actual effects. Is the viewing of sexually explicit material necessarily harmful, or can it be a helpful learning experience? An underlying question is posed by Dave Pomeroy in one of his thoughtful papers issued by the Emerging Technologies Information Service of the National Council's Communication Commission:

> Is explicitness (such as full or partial nudity) really the key problem? To what extent do suggestiveness (for example, afternoon soap operas) and titillation (for example, *Charlie's Angels*) communicate an understanding of sexuality which must be challenged or at least discussed from a values perspective?

He observes that Christians dealing with such issues

> have ranged from those who would deny much of the value and joy to be discovered in human sexuality to those who embrace uncritically forms of sexual thinking and acting that

may ultimately prove to be dehumanizing. The Christian church should feel a special challenge to help people throughout society deal with this relatively new phenomenon in ways that reflect the biblical call to become a full, true humanity.

Viewing fictional sexual experiences can lead thoughtful Christians to examine our own attitudes. *What standards underly the actions portrayed? Do those actions appear to me to be leading toward human fulfillment? Do they have any bearing on a continuing relationship? How satisfied am I with my own standards compared with the fictional ones?*

Viewers are confronted by the necessity to decide for themselves whether "what everyone is doing" is a sufficient standard to live by. This is the same alarming dilemma posed by studies like the old Kinsey reports. The percentage of persons engaged in extramarital sexual relations does not affect the morality of the act. If recognizing the prevalence of sexual unfaithfulness affects our attitude toward it, we have a weak foundation for our faith. All sin is statistically normal: that is, frequent, but not normal in the sense of being ideal. Humans have many "normal" thoughts which do not become normative for conduct. The person who cannot distinguish between what is being done and what ought to be done needs to grow, and vicarious experiences may help rather than hinder this development.

Unfortunately most programs in the electronic media either fail to suggest Christian values or present them in an unfavorable light. Proponents of sexual license are portrayed as vivacious and enlightened, while representatives of religious points of view are caricatured as prudish and judgmental. Peer discussions offer an opportunity to correct this distortion.

Exploitation

The major purpose of most electronic media is to sell goods, and anything goes in the process. This is especially true in the commercials, whether for merchandise or political candidates. Advertisers try to connect their products with viewers' desires.

Most readers will be able to recall commercials using the following appeals:

- You can win your children's love by giving them a certain candy.
- You can avoid failure by using this product.
- You will be sexually irresistible if you use this deodorant, perfume, or whatever.
- You will be the envy of the neighborhood if you drive this car.
- You can borrow money, if necessary, to make this purchase because you deserve the best.

Confronting such a barrage, the individual can exercise freedom to ask: *What inclination of mine is being addressed to get me to buy this product?* Chances are, it can be identified as envy, covetousness, or some other inclination at odds with the scriptural description of a Christian. Other questions follow: *What use do I actually have for the product? How much do I know about its quality?*

Many commercials do not pretend to make a rational appeal but use some sensational form of repetition in an attempt to bypass thought while implanting the brand name in a person's subconscious. Then, even if the commercial is offensive, the name will be recalled when the shopper walks the aisles of a supermarket and picks boxes from the shelves. Thus "Fill it to the rim with Brim" is obnoxiously unforgettable. So is "Dee-eep heating," but this one failed with me because I cannot remember the name of the remarkable ointment associated with it. There is even experimentation with subliminal ads, spots flashed so quickly that they will only register in the subconscious.

Some commercials are demonstrably misleading. One spot boasted that it took four bowls of Cornflakes to equal the "vitamin nutrition" of the cereal Total. But vitamins are only one component of nutrition. *Consumer Reports* revealed that out of 32 ready-to-eat cereals, Total (and the similar Product 19) were among the *least* nutritious, even less than the sugary Apple Jacks and Fruit Loops. Informed consumers can resist Madison Avenue wiles simply by refusing to buy products advertised in this manner.

For irritating commercials technology provides an excellent antidote—the mute button. Remote control units are worth their cost by providing for this function to be exercised in comfort. The pauses for tuned-out commercials are remarkably refreshing.

These actions will influence advertising practices only if increasing numbers of consumers adopt them.

Political ads are often as exploitative as product advertising, making flimsy claims to win votes. The sad fact is that candidates have learned that they cannot tell the truth and be elected. One gubernatorial candidate, in the same year when most states were facing huge deficits, pledged to try to hold expenditures down but admitted in his ads, "If there's still a deficit and you still want potholes filled and decent schools and more jobs, you're talking state income tax. You can't have it both ways." He lost by a large margin. So long as audiences choose to be deceived, exploitation will flourish.

Entertainment series often take advantage of audiences by using cliff-hanging techniques at the end of programs. The shooting of J. R. Ewing was the most spectacular example, but when "Hill Street Blues" ended one program with a shot which appeared to be a suicide and news was released that the officer had not actually died, one critic wrote, "It's a hokey gimmick that may boost the show's ratings. I don't like to be manipulated. But I'm dying to know what happens."

Membership in the new audience is demanding. One means of cultivating more thoughtful discrimination is to demonstrate how programs are made. When audiences understand the use of tricks, special effects, and technical devices, they are less likely to be deceived. There can be voluntary "suspension of disbelief," essential for all drama, without actual exploitation.

News

Walter Cronkite, interviewed after retirement by Barbara Walters on ABC television, expressed the opinion that television news coverage is becoming more and more trivial, more and more abbreviated. He saw show business aspects crowding out serious news coverage.

Here again the industry would claim that it is only serving the public. Harry Reasoner of CBS explains that when a reporter presents "what you sincerely hope is a reasoned, instructive, thoughtful piece on the Middle East or Pakistan or Red China or the international monetary crisis . . . it is frequently like tossing a rock in a pond." But, Reasoner says, once when he did a piece on men wearing panty hose he got a lot of mail.

Discriminating viewers can probe their attention to news broadcasts. *Which items interest me most—the substantial and informative or the trivial and titillating? Which ones do I remember well enough to discuss with others? Have I ever expressed my preferences to station personnel?* If there is really dissatisfaction with news coverage, management should be told. Viewers can also register their convictions by watching the programs that go beyond happy talk. The battle for news audiences does include a concern for the educated and influential, among others. Broadcasters are sensitive to reports such as one recent study indicating that during the past 10 years the percentage of viewers having "a great deal of confidence in TV news" has dropped from 47 to 24.

In the early morning, for example, it was once recognized that the "Today" show carried less hard news than "CBS Morning News," but more than ABC's "Good Morning America." Such differences offer at least a limited opportunity for viewer discrimination. Even more important is supplementing TV news with newspapers, magazines, and public broadcasting offerings like the "McNeil Lehrer NewsHour" or radio's "All Things Considered."

Putting it all together

All people "are continually engaged in making sense out of the world about them," according to sociologist Dean C. Barnlund. Claiming that this is among the few universals that apply to humanity, he elaborates, "Although men may tolerate doubt, few can tolerate meaninglessness."

Meaning is most often expressed through stories—myths, epics, parables. Tales of struggle and survival deal dramatically with questions: Why are we here? Where are we going?

Communication scholar George Gerbner, among others, has concluded that television is the central story-telling medium of our time. He says, "Electronic stories have replaced the socializing role of the pre-industrial church; they create a cultural mythology that establishes the norms of approved behavior and belief."

In the 70s "M*A*S*H" stimulated Americans to sift through our post-Vietnam attitudes; "All in the Family" exposed every possible prejudice for examination, and the "Mary Tyler Moore Show" gingerly explored women's roles. In the 80s "Hill Street Blues" is a reminder that there are no simple answers to crime. Changes in popular series reflect something about society. Lee Rich, producer of both "The Waltons" and "Dallas," has said, " 'The Waltons' were right for the time. People were saying, 'That's my family,' or 'I wish that was my family!' 'Dallas,' " he said, "was a respite for the American public, a fantasy-land. We fulfilled the dreams of many people." It is significant to note that while "Dallas" has been popular in many countries it has been a bust in Japan, where the family feuding is not understood and is contrary to the nation's value system.

Our response to the world view in electronic fiction tells us something important about ourselves. *How do my goals resemble or differ from the ones featured in these dramas? Is the road to "success" portrayed accurately—in terms of the price to be paid and satisfaction received? What are the influences producing this kind of world?*

It is not only through actual dramas that the electronic media present stories as models of life. Sporting events, political contests, protest movements, and activities of celebrities also offer dramatic possibilities for discovering meaning in existence. For the dedicated football fan who identifies with a losing team, life can appear to have tragic dimensions. The Superbowl has become a national cultic holiday. Political campaigns have the flavor of Advent, the conventions and elections arouse more excitement than Pentecost, and the funerals of celebrities generate more reflection about death than the Passion season. The pervasive media translate public events into mass rituals which acquire a subtle significance. Christians, especially, have a responsibility to become aware of what is happening and relate such events to our own, often quite different value system.

Religious references

Value systems underlying popular programs in the mass media are unlikely to be Christian partly because their creators are probably not practicing Christians. A survey of influential TV writers and executives in Hollywood has shown that they are far less religious than the general public, "diverge sharply from traditional values . . . " and "have moved toward a markedly more secular orientation." The study published in *Popular Opinion* magazine reports that 45% of the 104 professionals interviewed say they have no religion and only 7% of the other 55% say they attend a religious service as often as once a month. Nearly all, however, have had a religious background.

Like other unchurched people, these artists continue a search for meaning which may be reflected in their creations. On an episode of "St. Elsewhere" an elderly doctor, depressed by the probable diagnosis of leukemia in a child, is sobered by the child's own belief in God. In the film *Oh God II* young Tracy challenges George Burns with the question, "Why do you let bad things happen?" and the answers make more sense than some sermons on the same theme. At least they deal seriously with the question.

Theologian Martin Marty, writing in *TV Guide*, lamented the fact that situation comedies almost never reflect the fact that religion plays an important part in the lives of most Americans. This omission is too bad, he said, because "if producers could learn to situate religion in their comedies, TV would be richer, religion might be more accessible and our world would be both funnier and more humane." He proposed that sitcoms focus on a character not professionally religious, one of "God's-at-the-same-time-serious-and-merry-people." Marty claimed that such programs would be "guaranteed to make us laugh, and to inspire us."

When "M*A*S*H" went on the air Father Mulcahy was little more than a clerical wimp. Through the years, however, the character developed into a perceptive, caring person with a fine sense of humor.

The "Star Wars" film series is a cosmic drama portraying the eternal battle between good and evil. Theologian Robert Short claims that such cinematic fantasies offer a substitute for a lost but needed faith. In brushing off God, people lose any "sense of an ultimate 'why' in life," he says, but still "need this encounter so desperately" that they are drawn to it in imaginary space adventures. He also points out the symbolic connections of *E.T.* with the life of Jesus. Each came from a mysterious beyond; the Establishment disbelieved and rejected him, yet he was innocent of any wrong; he epitomized love, performed miracles, lived, died, lived again, and ascended. The Catholic-educated scriptwriter, Melissa Mathison, has been quoted as saying that it wasn't until after the filming that she recognized similarities with the Jesus story.

All attempts to portray cosmic significance in human experience provide rich material for thoughtful discussion.

Occasionally a biblical drama is presented in the public media, but these seldom improve on the imagination of a reader. The worst boast of being faithful to Scripture, but since the biblical writings were not intended to be scripts for dramatic production the resulting dialog and actions appear to be contrived and stilted. To put flesh on the abbreviated biblical descriptions requires sanctified imagination. Instead, the results usually reveal imagination without sanctity or sanctity without imagination. Biblical epics therefore call for even more critical interpretation than purely secular productions.

Viewers of programs making religious references have many questions to ask, such as the following:

- What impression is given of God? Angry avenger? Power pipeline? Sanctified slot machine? Insurance company? Suffering servant?
- Does God appear to be a comforting or disturbing force?

- Are the human characters interested in resources beyond themselves?
- Is there recognition of pervasive evil in the world?
- Does there appear to be any basis for hope in life?
- How is the church portrayed? Outdated and irrelevant? Unfaithful to its founder? Caring?

Special contributions

The public media can give special impetus to certain efforts and causes by focusing attention on pressing issues and needs. The new audience should be prepared to take advantage of all such opportunities.

The NBC movie "M.A.D.D.: Mothers Against Drunk Drivers" raised public awareness nationwide and caused a surge of interest in the organization fighting the plague of alcohol-related accidents.

Another NBC movie "Adam" portrayed the desperate search of a couple for their kidnapped son. Its poignant reality helped in the passage of legislation authorizing greater cooperation from law enforcement agencies in the search for missing children.

The controversial film about nuclear holocaust, "The Day After," did little except demonstrate the obvious, that nuclear war would be apocalyptic, but it did stimulate thoughtful exchange about what should be done to avoid global catastrophe. This, according to director Nicholas Meyer, was the intention. Before the telecast Meyer said, "We're going after those who haven't formed an opinion. The most troublesome aspect of the nuclear issue is that people can't bear to think about it. . . . All I want is for the movie to inspire debate."

We know that mere portrayal of evils is not therapeutic. After West German audiences flocked to see a film depicting the horrible life of a teenaged drug addict in Berlin, supporting her habit by prostitution, there were fears that the young woman was becoming a cult heroine and possibly a role model. Young visitors who formerly asked to see the Berlin Wall were found looking for the subway station haunted by the film's leading character.

Discriminating viewing in groups can provide a different frame of reference and the new electronic media underscore this possibility. Harvard Professor James Q. Wilson has described a process for educating young people to be capable parents. He attributes most delinquency to the prevalence of bad parental practices and maintains that the major problem is overcoming resistance to adopting common-sense techniques. He believes this can be accomplished. "Suppose," he says, "the techniques of scoring behavior from videotapes of actual families in trouble were taught in school, using the same techniques researchers now rely on—the engrossing paraphernalia of hand-held computer terminals and video displays with which the Pac-Man generation has become so familiar. Suppose the changes in behavior that occur as a result of adopting sensible parenting techniques could be seen (on a TV set) by young people. It is conceivable that they might find this experience more interesting and this information more useful than what they often get from lectures they are now obliged to get on sex education or personal hygiene, to say nothing of courses in civics or woodworking."

Someone is bound to suggest that thoughtful discussion of video presentations will destroy the enjoyment usually associated with viewing. This need not happen under capable leadership. In fact, such exchange can enhance the pleasure of the experience.

Discriminating viewing is also important in the support of good programming. Station executives should be informed when viewers, especially in numbers, regard a program as valuable. Socially conscious executives are always under pressure not to take risks with series which do not immediately rank high in the ratings. They need encouragement from groups who believe a program has basic values which will help it attract an audience of respectable size if given time.

There is evidence that candidates for a more discriminating audience are waiting to be mobilized. A Television Audience Assessment Study made public in 1983 asserted that TV viewers had become less attentive to the programs they were watching. In a 1984 *USA Today* poll of television viewing habits, 59% of those surveyed rated regular network programs as only fair to poor. One educational project, *Television Awareness Training,* is being carried on by church groups in an effort to encourage critical viewing.

Without active response from the nucleus of a new audience, programming in the popular media is likely to get worse rather than better. The public interest has only feeble representation at present in Washington, New York, and Hollywood. We will take one final look at what, if anything, can be done about that.

Participation in 10
Reformation

Like all human creations, the American system of broadcasting has strengths and weaknesses, and requires periodic modification. As Christians who acknowledge that even the church benefits from continuing reformation, we have a responsibility to participate in the reformation of all of our institutions. This is especially true of agencies controlling the electronic media which exert such an influence on society.

The public interest

The broadcasting system in the United States was not established for the entertainment of the 18-49-year-old consumers. The Communications Act of 1934 was based on the conviction that the airwaves belong to everyone and that users of them are trustees. Licenses were to be granted on condition that broadcasters serve "the public interest, convenience, and necessity." The Federal Communications Commission was created to manage the system and to see that the public interest is served.

The term "public interest" is subject to varying interpretations, but over the years the concept has been defined by the courts and FCC to include at least these provisions:

● that a fundamental purpose of broadcasting is to foster informed public opinion through the dissemination of news and opinion concerning events and issues of the day.

● that in order for the public to be fully informed, the stations must offer holders of the various contrasting viewpoints reasonable opportunities to be heard.

● that broadcasting is primarily a local institution and that broadcasters, as public trustees, must work at determining the needs of their communities and program to serve those needs.

Gradually it became apparent that if the public interest was to be respected, the public would need to be heard. In 1963 a House of Representatives Report on the FCC stated: "Under our system, the interests of the public are dominant. The commercial needs of licensed broadcasters and advertisers must be integrated into those of the public." The report went on to say that citizens have a duty to be concerned with local and network services and that they need not feel "that in taking a hand in broadcasting they are unduly interfering in the private business affairs of others. On the contrary, their interest in programming is direct and their responsibilities important. They are the owners of the channels of television—indeed of all broadcasting."

In the United States "the owners of the channels" have had little to say about broadcasting; the licensed operators of equipment and the unlicensed networks, advertisers, and producers have made nearly all the important decisions.

In other democracies different patterns have been followed. Nowhere have commercial interests been given a blank check. The British Broadcasting Corporation is an "autonomous public corporation," neither a tool of the government nor an agency entirely free of public supervision. The commercial television companies in Britain are subject to much more regulation than in the United States. They are also required to contribute to the cost of operating a separate program service, Channel 4, with a schedule comparable to PBS in the United States. Elsewhere in the Commonwealth similar policies prevail. Periodically, as in Canada, for example, public commissions reexamine the system and make recommendations for changes to preserve consideration of public interest.

In Scandinavia, France, and Germany broadcasting is generally under government auspices, with protection against political partisanship. Recognizing the pervasive social influence of the media, no group is allowed to exploit them for exclusively private purposes. The coming of cable and satellites complicates their situation, but national communication authorities deliberate at length on means of protecting the interests of the public.

In the Netherlands there is a unique arrangement whereby various groups, including churches and labor unions, have control over substantial segments of broadcast time.

Our American system has the advantage of minimizing government restriction on the freedom of broadcasters and it encourages initiative that results in a great quantity of programs, available without direct charge to listener-viewers. Its weakness is its dependence for representation of the public interest on an agency, the Federal Communications Commission, which has proven to be unequal to the task.

Erosion of representation

The Federal Communications Commission is under enormous pressure, much of it from the multimillion dollar electronic industry. Some courageous commissioners have tried to defend the public interest against the tides of commercial domination, but the floodwalls have been cracking and are in danger of being swept away. Commission decisions often reflect more sympathy with industry than awareness of social impact. Congress is reluctant to intervene in FCC actions because elected representatives are so dependent on the media for assistance in relating to their constituency.

Networks and stations have come to believe that they have little to fear from public criticism. Already in 1966 Warren Burger, later to become Chief Justice, said, "After nearly five decades of operation the broadcast industry does not seem to have grasped the simple fact that a broadcast license is a public trust subject to termination for breach of duty."

In 1974, as a result of organized pressure from parents upset by the commercial exploitation of children's programs, the FCC adopted a Policy Statement attempting to set desirable standards. In 1979, when a special task force concluded that TV broadcasters were not satisfying the goals of the 1974 statement, a new rule-making procedure was launched, but in 1983 the Commission not only failed to strengthen the 1974 statement but virtually repudiated it. This was clearly in line with the move away from any meaningful regulation.

Newsweek critic Harry F. Waters, under a headline, "Kidvid: A National Disgrace," wrote:

> There once was a time when the network rulers of children's television dispensed bread as well as circuses. For every zap-pow fribble, there were equal servings of redeeming food for thought. The networks kept that salutary balance not so much because they cared for junior America's mental health—but mostly they dreaded the wrath of a watchful regulatory agency in Washington. . . . [Then, Waters noted, came deregulation] and the networks were free to indulge their greed . . . and the children awoke one day to find their looking glass world inundated by a tide of sludge.

The expansion of electronic facilities can be used as an ideological support for deregulation, allowing only the marketplace to govern mass media programming. Historically the scarcity of radio and TV channels was cited as the reason for more public supervision of these media than of print. Now, with the projected increase in stations, cable, and even satellite systems, this argument no longer seems applicable. The claim, however, that anybody can now operate a TV station is a farce because of the enormous investment involved.

Most communities will not enjoy more diversity of services for many years. Even then, there is no assurance, in the light of economic realities, that diversity will mean more than increased numbers of affluent operators distributing more and more of the same commercial fare.

Above all, the electronic media are distinctive because they use the airwaves, a public resource. Like forests, water, and highways, the broadcasting spectrum serves a common purpose and must be regulated for the common good. In setting policies for radio, TV, satellite, and cable, government is dealing with intrusive media which, unlike print, pervade society, reaching across boundaries and into homes. Their potential influence must be recognized and their functions extended beyond sales to service.

Creeping commercialism

Herbert Hoover, in 1924, said, "I believe the quickest way to kill broadcasting would be to use it for direct advertising." The predicted demise has certainly been delayed, but symptoms of a debilitating illness are appearing. A survey by the National Citizens Committee for Broadcasting found that 80% of the respondents felt commercials interrupted programs too frequently and 55% claimed not to pay attention to them. The time devoted to ads has increased steadily with the willingness of sponsors to pay. How far can this trend go before the media are discredited? Are there any limits to what the audience will endure? It takes a long time for public opinion to generate concerted response but, meanwhile, sustaining services, including ecumenical religious programs, are being squeezed off the air.

It should be possible, we have observed, to move religious programs canceled from over-the-air stations to public access channels on cable. This, however, is likely to result in sharp reduction of audience. Even programs for particular groups have a better chance to attract listener-viewers on the more popular channels. In Britain, when an archeology program with an audience of 100,000 was shifted to a more specialized channel, the figure dropped to 9000.

Marketplace limits

More serious are reservations with the basic concept of marketplace standards for public media. Under our economic system the ability to make and sell whatever people will buy has created an abundance of products. This industrial/commercial process, however, has had undesirable side effects requiring correction. Exploitation of workers led to protection for unions and child labor laws. Pollution of air and water, plus dumping of hazardous wastes, made it obvious that environmental protection is a necessary governmental function. The old hedge, "let the buyer beware," has been recognized as inadequate even by Better Business Bureaus. But broadcasting appears to be hankering after the days of the industrial "robber barons." At the very time when many large corporations are becoming more accountable in terms of social influence, broadcasting is being allowed to move in the opposite direction. The Carnegie Commission on the Future of Public Broadcasting said:

> American radio and television are not just instruments of the marketplace; they are social tools of revolutionary importance. If these media are permitted to assume a wholly commercial character, the entire cultural and social apparatus of the nation will become transformed by what may already have become the dominant mode of the electronic media in the United States: the merchandizing of consciousness.

Socially conscious industry executives recognize blind spots in a marketplace approach to electronic policy. Joel Chaseman, president of *Post-Newsweek* Stations, Inc., has said:

> The let-the-marketplace-decide approach is wrong in principle. It is clearly not in the public interest for spectrum to be assigned among potential uses or users on the basis of the highest bid, without regard for the nature or importance of the use itself. . . .

Referring to proposals for direct broadcast from satellite to home, Chaseman commented:

> What marketplace is this? It costs approximately 350 million dollars from design of satellite through the launch of space vehicle to daily operation, not to mention the purchase or lease by each household or business of an earth station costing several hundred dollars plus an additional monthly charge. A very special marketplace indeed, competitive only to those who can afford a billion-dollar entry fee. . . . Deregulation cannot become a synonym for abdication, especially when the public interest so obviously calls for service which is free to all."

Cable, satellite, computers, and combinations of the media increase possibilities for misuse as well as use. In Italy, when local commercial TV stations were allowed to begin operating without regulation, one began showing hard-core adult movies like *Deep Throat*. Another station introduced striptease elements into a game show and soon nudity and pornography became common on Italian television.

To reply, "It can't happen here," makes no sense to Christians, who have a realistic understanding of human nature. Sexually stimulating messages are already being offered by telephone in this country. In 1983 *High Society Magazine* was providing such a service used by 600,000 callers per day, netting $56,000 for the phone company and $12,000 for the magazine. Sexually explicit programs on cable have precipitated legal battles in various communities.

The worst drives out the best

Exploitation of sex is only one indication of marketplace orientation. Manufacturers of quality products perform a useful service in marketing them, but extreme pressure for sales records calls for merchandising efforts which bypass ethics. Appeals to the worst in human self-interest are the easiest path to sales and the easiest way to build audiences. As the marketplace idea becomes dominant, even hesitant attempts to deal with human reality in situation comedies are losing out. A *Newsweek* writer, mourning the demise of the Bunkers, Mary Richards, and Hawkeye Pierce, said that in their place "glitters the age of tinsel: jejune, who's necking-at-the-drive-in sitcoms aimed at pubescents and banal, boardroom-to-bedroom melodramas designed for adults with easily titillated libidos or two-digit IQs."

When "Hill Street Blues" slipped behind "Knots Landing" there were pressures to spice up the show. The leading character was fired (temporarily) and came close to resuming his alcoholism, his wife received death threats, and the girlfriend of another police officer became pregnant.

Creative artists working in the electronic media do not hesitate to admit that the marketplace quest for the largest possible audience has deprived the American public of potential values in television. Larry Gelbart of "M*A*S*H" has said that people developing programs for television "are often invited really to leave their brains and their hearts and their feelings outside the door." Writer Abby Mann, with *Judgment at Nuremberg* among his credits, reflecting on the wealth of talented writers, directors, and actors in Hollywood, said, "I just can't help thinking what a pity it is that we don't have a medium that calls out for the best, but calls out for the worst in them." David Rintels, who wrote *Clarence Darrow*, has commented on the importance of television, "It is for many a source of information about the real world. But the message they are getting is, I think, not an honest message."

NBC's late night news effort, "Overnight," was never criticized but simply canceled. Evidently it did not attract enough viewers. Producers mused, "Being good is not enough."

Policy and power

The U.S. government has never formulated a clear, comprehensive policy concerning electronic media. This is not surprising since we also lack long-range policies to deal with energy, the environment, and urban affairs. Frequent political changes result in shifts of direction. New problems, multiplied by the development of new media, are treated on an ad hoc basis.

On all issues involving mass communication, powerful forces are marshalled on behalf of industry interests. Networks are now linked in conglomerates with banks and armament manufacturers. Representation of the public interest is unlikely to be organized and financed in so impressive a manner, but this does not necessarily indicate disinterest.

In Sweden in the mid-70s, the public was invited to participate in the formation of a national energy policy. To assure that participants would be informed, a 10-hour course of study was offered, with the understanding that recommendations from persons taking the course would be considered. Instead of a projected figure of 10,000, more than 75,000 enrolled.

Traditionally in the U.S. it is possible for informed citizens to affect the system. One individual, to be sure a New York lawyer, John F. Banzaf III, took action which eventually resulted in the banning of more than 200 million dollars worth of cigarette advertising on television and radio in 1971. Five years earlier Banzaf requested free time, under the Fairness Doctrine, from New York station WCBS-TV to reply to cigarette commercials. Denied this permission, Banzaf complained to the FCC on the basis that promotion of a proven health hazard on TV and radio was a controversial issue of public importance. The FCC supported his contention and ruled that all stations would have to carry one antismoking spot for every three cigarette commercials. Later Congress went even further and passed the Public Health Smoking Act, banning cigarette advertising on broadcast stations. Printed media were exempt from the ban because they are not licensed in the public interest.

Now, as we have noted, the trend toward deregulation and away from such provisions as the Fairness Doctrine makes such actions improbable. Congress is still a last resort, but the public interest must compete for attention with the influential lobbying of private power.

The record of American churches in voicing concern over use of the airwaves is spotty. The most spectacular effort to influence the FCC demonstrated both organizational strength and ignorance. In 1975 a legal document known as the Lansman-Milam petition was filed with the FCC, requesting a review of the policy whereby sectarian religious groups, who were eligible for regular commercial licenses, should also be allowed to hold FM noncommercial licenses. Independent evangelical groups misinterpreted the petition to propose elimination of religious broadcasting, and even linked it mistakenly with atheist Madalyn Murray O'Hair. Counter petition drives spawned thousands of letters and, even though the FCC promptly in 1975 rejected the Lansman-Milam petition, letters continued to flow. After a few years the FCC set aside a room to hold the letters and stopped attempting to reply. It was clear that churches could generate protest correspondence but it was also, unfortunately, obvious that the writers were so misinformed that their views were unworthy of consideration.

Landmark case

Mainline churches, led by the Office of Communication of the United Church of Christ, originally directed by Everett C. Parker, have been more credible and therefore more influential in dealing with the FCC. William F. Fore has been an able representative of the Communication Commission of the NCC in frequent Washington appearances.

A landmark case was the one which led to the loss of license of the Lamar Life Insurance Company to operate WLBT-TV in Jackson, Mississippi. Charging that the station was guilty of racial and religious discrimination, the United Church of Christ Office of Communication challenged WLBT's license renewal before the FCC. The Commission ruled that the challenging organization was not a "party in interest" but the case was appealed to the United States Court of Appeals in the District of Columbia and, in a historic ruling, the FCC was ordered to allow the Office of Communication to participate in public hearings on the renewal issue. Warren E. Burger, then a Circuit Court Judge, said,

> In order to safeguard the public interest in broadcasting . . . we hold that some "audience participation" must be allowed in license renewal proceedings. . . . Such community organizations as civic associations, professional societies, unions, churches, and educational institutions or associations might well be helpful to the commission. These groups . . . usually concern themselves with a wide range of community problems and tend to be representative of broad as distinguished from narrower interests, public as distinguished from private or commercial interests.

In the WLBT case the FCC conducted a hearing and still granted the station its renewal, but the petitioners again appealed to the court which unanimously reversed the commission and revoked the license. The station was subsequently licensed to a corporation with majority black ownership.

The petition to deny a station's license is an extreme example of community action, requiring major expenditures of time and money. The precedent established in the WLBT case, however, also makes possible less drastic action to bring about change.

In another instance the Office of Communication of the United Church of Christ moved from litigation to negotiation in improving conditions for blacks at TV station KTAL in Texarkana. In a petition to deny license renewal, the station was charged with egregious racial discrimination in its broadcasts and in its hiring practices. Before a hearing was scheduled, the station agreed to negotiate and the parties reached a settlement that improved KTAL's employment of blacks and its service to the Texarkana area.

Various organizations are at work attempting to represent the public interest in the communications field. They persist despite the unfavorable governmental climate of the 80s.

Mainline churches, led by the United Church of Christ, have spearheaded a public (consumer) media reform movement. Action for Children's Television (ACT) is a national organization with chapters in most major cities. In consultation with educators and child-development specialists ACT attempts to influence programs and advertising directed to children by dealing with networks, the FCC, and the Federal Trade Commission. Other active agencies include the National Citizens Committee for Broadcasting, a Ralph Nader organization, and Accuracy in Media. The American Medical Association and the national Parent Teacher Association occasionally lend support in strategic efforts related to issues such as excessive violence.

The Telecommunications Consumer Coalition was formed to deal with questions arising from new electronic developments. Founded by the United Church of Christ, the Consumer Federation of America, and Consumers Union, TCC is an excellent clearing house for current information concerning regulatory and legislative issues in telecommunications. The National Council of Churches' Cable TV and Emerging Technologies Service periodically issues informative documents.

Regulatory reform

Recognizing that the public has had little influence on national communication policy in the past, what hope is there for more effective representation in a future with even more complex issues? Regulatory reform will not come easily, but liberty is never retained without eternal vigilance. Perhaps a significant number of Christian citizens feel like the disillusioned anchorman in the movie, *Network*: "I'm mad as hell. I'm not going to take this anymore." At least there are now agencies to inform ordinary citizens concerning pending issues, and members of most denominations can turn to their communication executives to advise them in positions of advocacy with government officials.

Many serious questions related to the electronic age face the FCC and, eventually, Congress, where rewrites of the 1934 Communications Act are under consideration. How far should deregulation go? Should the FCC be allowed to abdicate all responsibility for assuring the existence of quality and social purpose in media programming? How should the rights to use domestic satellites be allocated? Should the Fairness Doctrine be retained? Should equal time and fairness rules apply to cable? How much control should local communities have over cable franchises? What restrictions should be exercised over multiple ownership of broadcasting stations and cable systems? Should new broadcasting stations be licensed by lottery or by comparative hearings? What procedures should be followed in license renewals? What protection can be instituted to guard against invasion of privacy from the new computerized media? Should frequencies originally dedicated exclusively to educational use (Instructional Television Fixed Service) be released for other purposes? Can media time be distributed more fairly among political candidates? Should any limits be placed on the percentage of broadcast time devoted to commercials? Still other questions involve network syndication rights, cable copyrights, and permission for commercials on public television.

There are so many ramifications to most of these issues and treatment of them changes so radically with each passing month that any attempt at specific analysis in a book might be meaningless by the time of its publication. There are, however, two general principles, one or both of which are likely to apply to each specific problem under consideration.

Restore balance

The first is a determination to restore a balance between marketplace forces and the broader public interest. The FCC has never been overly strong, but there have been times when that agency has kept in check the worst dangers from commercial excesses. Now reform movements must begin by bucking a trend toward complete deregulation.

In the past, broadcasting stations were at least required to put in writing their intentions to perform a service to their community, thus establishing a standard for accountability at license renewal time. Any dilution of this minimal provision represents a loss to the public.

An alternative proposal, submitted by Everett Parker to the FCC, would establish an operational standard requiring:

1. programming which affords opportunity for self-expression to persons and groups in the service area;

2. programming which gives information about matters of particular interest or concern in the service area; and

3. programming presented to serve the needs of nonprofit and governmental organizations in the service area.

Such standards are not likely to be adopted or enforced unless members of the FCC represent more than private interests. There should be more expression of public concern when appointments are under consideration. Whatever the makeup of the Commission, congressional review is important. This is especially true at a time when rewrites of the Communications Act of 1934 are being submitted. Elected officials are more likely than appointees to give attention to thoughtful presentations by constituents. It may be time to pursue again a proposal which emerges periodically from deliberations over the media, the establishment of a public advisory commission to review annually the workings of our system and make recommendations to Congress and the FCC.

Genuine diversity

A second principle is the preservation and extension of genuine diversity in electronic services.

Deregulation in favor of the marketplace principle may increase the quantity of services while decreasing diversity because commercial monopolies are allowed to develop.

In the United States the concept of diversity in communication is upheld by the First Amendment, guaranteeing both the right to speak or publish and the right to hear or read. Both freedom to express and freedom to know are defended. In the post-1984 age both of these rights may be exercised primarily through two-way, electronic communications—a television set linked to a computer by a keyboard. In planning for the future it is essential that this system be accessible to as many different sources of information and entertainment as possible. John Wicklein, author of *Electronic Nightmare: The New Communications and Freedom*, has commented on this need:

> The most important thing we can do is prevent monopoly control of content in the new system by a national carrier or by local system operators. . . . We should also be concerned about *de facto* control of content by large information conglomerates which, through their marketing power, combined with their ownership of distribution media, may be able to dominate the information marketplace.

Wicklein does not believe that diversity is going to be guaranteed by dependence on the marketplace. He says, "The information and entertainment supplied by such a profit system has to go where the money is—there can be little concern for providing services to the public that do not return a profit."

Wicklein concludes that the best way to build provision for diversity into the structure is to separate content from technology in the new Communication Act. He would favor treating systems for such services as satellite, videotext, and even local cable as common carriers, operating the distribution systems technologically but having no responsibility for programming. He acknowledges that it is late to apply this principle to cable, but proposes that systems already operating be required to lease some channels to other information providers.

For genuine diversity, including expression of creativity in efforts to serve society, extension of public broadcasting to the newer forms of telecommunication is highly desirable. The Carnegie Commission on the Future of Public Broadcasting proposed a comprehensive system for program delivery, saying, "Our history demonstrates that marketplace considerations sometimes do not encourage the full development and application of techniques and innovations which benefit all sectors of the public. Removed from the dictates of the marketplace, public broadcasting can play an important leadership role in bringing the benefits of the new technology to the public."

In America we were slow to recognize the importance of maintaining a strong publicly oriented radio and TV element to balance the commercial component in our national system. Financial entrepreneurs always seem to be more bold than educational innovators. In the new electronic services such as cable there ought to be public operators in some cities setting a pattern for comparison with private operators elsewhere.

At the very least, public access channels should be retained, even though some communities are slow in utilizing them. Cooperative administration of the channels may be necessary.

Censorship?

In our discussion of needed reforms we have emphasized the positive—making provision for diversity and presentations that are in the public interest. But what about the prospect that unrestrained marketplace forces will increase such negative output as pornography and obscenity? Should there be restrictive legislation?

In a democracy censorship, in the strict sense of prior restraint by government, is almost limited to material which, if distributed, would endanger society.

Even this criterion is subject to interpretation because one of the functions of the media is to provide information on which society's decisions are based. When the *New York Times* learned about the impending Bay of Pigs invasion of Cuba, the story was withheld at the request of President Kennedy. After the debacle Kennedy is reported to have wished that the *Times* had turned him down, thus aborting the ill-fated attempt. But in that case the *Times* could have been accused of national disloyalty.

There can be legislation against obscenity. The Supreme Court has said: "This much has been categorically settled by the Court, that obscene material is unprotected by the First Amendment."

Judges and juries have been directed to ask:

● whether the work depicts or describes, in a patently offensive way, sexual conduct specifically defined as illegal;

● whether the work, taken as a whole, lacks serious literary, political, or scientific value;

● whether to the average person, applying contemporary community standards, the dominant theme of the material taken as a whole appeals to prurient interests.

All such definitions are difficult to apply. Who is an average person? Is there agreement on contemporary community standards? Who is qualified to determine the dominant theme of a work of art? Who is to say whether the interests aroused are prurient?

In some communities it may be possible to enforce restrictions on occasional media productions. There must be minimal protection against excesses by unscrupulous profiteers who would exploit the immature and unstable. But experience indicates that censorship is usually counterproductive. Human nature being what it is, audiences are increased by bans. As we have indicated in Chapter 9, Christians ought to be able to grow and learn from exposure even to forthright portrayals of evil.

This does not mean that nothing can be done about the distribution of offensive presentations. Operators of the media exercise more influence than government anyway, and a good relationship with some of them may be productive.

Friendly adversaries

In proposing reformation of the American telecommunication system it is easy to give the impression that the public interest is diametrically opposite the financial well-being of the industry. This is not true, especially in the long run. Commercial operators have a major contribution to make to the American system, provided there is recognition that profit-making is not the only function of the media. Public approval is also important for the continuing well-being of the industry. In setting policies, representatives of the public and private interests may be friendly adversaries rather than antagonists. Both sides can, for example, confer on the formulation of such policies as those providing for public service uses of communications satellites.

Bureaucratic demands by past Federal Communications Commissions for voluminous record keeping have increased the natural opposition of broadcasters to all regulation. A reasonable amount of regulation, however, is in the best interests of both the public and socially conscious broadcasters. Without any enforced standards the most exploitative commercial interests could become dominant, forcing more ethical operators to compete on the worst terms for existence.

Beyond minimal legislated restrictions there is need for self-regulation. Fred Friendly, former CBS news president, has pointed to the difference between what a journalist has a right to do and what is the right thing to do. This principle can be extended to other programs, and the relationship of friendly adversaries should help to make the distinction. On the local level, especially, media owners and operators, often committed Christians themselves, are responsive to public opinion.

Media professionals often join in questioning whether children should be exposed to all of the world's evils at an early age. Al Goldstein, who admits that his own cable program "Midnight

Blue" is "clearly unsuitable for children," argues that no such program should be scheduled before late at night. He claims to be "shocked and angered by the programming of Home Box Office and Cinemax . . . wolfishly exposing young children to gore and explicit violence by showing repulsive horror movies at a time when most children are awake and watching TV."

Unfortunately, groups critical of the media are often guilty of such unreasonable, naive condemnation that their opinions are disregarded. Some Christians would censor all depictions of sin, overlooking vivid reports of sinful actions in the Bible. Contradictory positions are not uncommon. Members of the National Coalition on Television Violence (NCTV) thought they were making progress with the networks until the Moral Majority, apparently more opposed to sex than violence, welcomed programs condemned by NCTV. The Moral Majority supported two very violent shows because of their apparent emphasis on law and order.

Friendly criticism, then, should be based on more than a puritanical view of sex or the arithmetic of violence. There should be support and promotion of good programs and encouragement of advertisers who pay for them. When one insurance company sponsored a series of high quality, hour-long specials, executives reduced commercial time from nine to six minutes and limited themselves to informational ads. Such an effort is worthy of commendation.

Boycotts

One device for expressing dissatisfaction with media performance is the boycott. When applied indiscriminately—turn off the TV set for one day or one week—it means nothing except, perhaps, as an exercise in self-discipline. It makes no more sense than to say, because there are hideous paperbacks, I'll read nothing for a week.

Directed to advertisers, a boycott can have significance. Knowing that some advertisers plan to irritate listener-viewers, counting on them to forget the irritation but remember the brand

name, a different reaction can be taught. We can learn to remember both the irritation and the brand name and refuse to
buy the product. Even some advertising executives expect this
to happen eventually. John O'Toole, chairman of one of the 10
largest advertising firms in the nation, blasts repetitious and intrusive ads. Referring to "Ring around the collar" and "Please
don't squeeze the Charmin" campaigns, he says,

> These commercials insult my intelligence both as a consumer
> and as an advertising professional. . . . The consumer is re-
> sentful. . . . He is insulted at being talked down to. These
> commercials evoke a negative attitude toward advertising,
> which is detrimental to all of us in this business.

Refusing to buy products advertised in so offensive a manner
cannot be compared with censorship. Advertisers are free to air
their commercials but consumers likewise are free to refuse to
be duped by them.

It is increasingly difficult to apply commercial boycotts to specific programs because most broadcasts now have multiple sponsors. Generally, however, advertisers do have the option of
indicating where their commercials are to be placed and they
should be urged to consider when identification with a particular
program is in line with their own views of serving the public.

Boycott of products advertised on offensive programs is simply
a commercial lever to influence a system with a strong commercial
makeup. Complaints by network executives concerning this practice received a strong reply from columnist George Will, not
noted for opposition to private enterprise. He wrote:

> Networks live lives of cheerful, not to say brazen contradic-
> tion. They trumpet their prowess at causing people to buy
> material goods: Hey, we can modify behavior in 30 seconds.
> Yet they deny, or disclaim responsibility for, the coarsening
> consequences of hour after hour of base programs. . . . It is
> hard (and hardly obligatory) to credit the sincerity of people
> who shout "Censorship!"—with that word's connotation of
> coercive state actions—when people are simply planning to
> practice selective buying of beer and panty hose.

Will claimed that networks "are turning airwaves into Love Canals of the mind" and appealed,

Let's all get started. Dial soap helps sponsor the execrable "Flamingo Road." Aren't you glad you don't use Dial? Don't you wish nobody did?

Global responsibility

The American electronic industry is accused of misinforming and corrupting people beyond national borders because U.S. productions have extensive worldwide distribution. With their technological and economic advantages, American media tend to exert disproportionate influence in less developed countries.

It is certainly true that many of the U.S. entertainment programs aired abroad are less than admirable. This so-called cultural imperialism, however, has a similarity to prostitution and the drug traffic, in that guilt is not lodged exclusively in the party marketing the services. In some countries restrictions have been placed on the scheduling of programs produced elsewhere. In Britain, for example, not more that 14% of TV program material may come from foreign sources. One TV network in Brazil produces more than 85% of its own programs and reaches 95% of the 80 million Brazilian television viewers.

Domestic production does not automatically correct the problem. American programs are seductively popular precisely because they appeal to universal elements in human nature and homeland replacements do not necessarily bring about improvement.

It must also be admitted that the picture of the Third World presented in our news media is badly distorted. The image of the United States presented by most media in the developing countries is equally garbled. Journalist N. Balakrishnan, writing in the news magazine *Far Eastern Economic Review* of Hong Kong, says:

It is time that Third World journalists engaged in some introspection and took a critical look at how they cover the "enemy" instead of being so quick to cast the first stone. In fact, if one were to use the same criteria to evaluate news about the U.S. appearing in the Third World media and news about the Third World appearing in the U.S., it is likely that the U.S. would emerge as the more injured party.

From all sides there is agreement that there is need for improvement in the international system of information exchange. This has led to the proposal for a New World Information and Communication Order. There are widely different ideas as to what should be new. The Western democracies favor the free flow of information, but Eastern and less developed countries fear what they regard as violation of their borders by unrestricted global transmission.

Of all agencies interested in this problem, the Christian church, with representation in East and West, North and South, should be able to sense a commonality of interests and recommend policies which facilitate the search for truth through responsible exercise of freedom. This will involve being on guard against exploitative actions of transnational corporations. At the same time, repressive procedures of governments on both the political left and right must be resisted.

On a related issue there is a more obvious opportunity for Christians to take a position of advocacy in international deliberations. Allocations for broadcasting and satellite channels are coordinated by a United Nations Agency, the International Telecommunications Union. With the expansion of electronic media there is increasing demand for frequencies, and agreements are negotiated at World Administrative Radio Conferences. The more affluent nations argue that they should be given preference in this distribution because they will make immediate use of the frequencies. If this view prevails, the less-developed countries will be left out in the cold when they become able to operate satellites and extend their communication systems. This is clearly an instance when Western Christians should express their solidarity with brothers and sisters in Africa, Asia, and Latin America by appealing to our own government to recognize the legitimate needs of others.

"Ordinary people," members of typical local congregations, may feel inadequate to enter into discussions about issues facing the United Nations or even the Federal Communications Commission and Congress. There is great danger in the fact that nearly everyone feels this way. But there is great opportunity in the fact that a few thoughtful, well-informed citizens may therefore be unusually influential. For Christians willing to do their homework, there is plenty to do both with and about the media.

For Further Reading

Armstrong, Ben. *The Electric Church*. Nashville: Thomas Nelson, Inc., 1979. (Out of print.)

Barnouw, Eric. *A History of Broadcasting in the U.S. to 1933.* Vol. 1. *A Tower in Babel.* New York: Oxford University Press, 1966.

Barnouw, Eric. *The Sponsor: Notes on a Modern Potentate.* New York: Oxford University Press, 1978.

Barnouw, Eric. *The Tube of Plenty: The Evolution of American Television.* New York: Oxford University Press, 1975.

Brown, Les. *Keeping Your Eye on Television.* New York: The Pilgrim Press, 1979.

Bryant, Jennings and Anderson, Daniel R., editors. *Children's Understanding of Television: Research on Attention and Comprehension.* New York: Academic Press, 1983.

Charren, Peggy and Sandler, Martin W. *Changing Channels: Living (Sensibly) with Television.* Reading, Mass.: Addison-Wesley Publishing Company, 1983.

Cole, Barry and Oettinger, Mal. *Reluctant Regulators: The FCC and the Broadcast Audience.* Reading, Mass.: Addison-Wesley Publishing Company, 1978.

Comstock, George, Steven Chaffee, Natan Katzman, Maxwell McCombs, and Donald Roberts. *Television and Human Behavior.* New York: Columbia University Press, 1978.

Cox, Harvey. *The Seduction of the Spirit: The Use and Misuse of People's Religion.* London: Wildwood House, 1974.

Fore, William. *Image and Impact: How Man Comes Through in Mass Media*. New York: Friendship Press, 1970. (Out of print.)

Gerbner, George, ed. *Mass Media Policies in Changing Cultures*. New York: Wiley, 1977.

Hadden, Jeffrey K. and Swann, Charles E. *Prime Time Preachers: The Rising Power of Televangelism*. Reading, Mass.: Addison-Wesley Publishing Company, 1981.

Hoover, Stewart M. *The Electronic Giant*. Elgin, Ill.: The Brethren Press, 1981.

Horsfield, Peter. *Religious Television: The Experience in America*. New York: Longman, 1984.

McLuhan, Marshall. *Understanding Media: The Extension of Man*. New York: McGraw-Hill, 1964.

Mander, Jerry. *Four Arguments for the Elimination of Television*. New York: Quill, 1978.

Marc, David. *Democratic Vistas*. Philadelphia: University of Pennsylvania Press, 1984.

Marty, Martin. *The Improper Opinion*. Philadelphia: Westminster Press, 1961. (Out of print.)

Muggeridge, Malcolm. *Christ and the Media*. Sevenoaks, Kent: Hodder and Stoughton, 1977.

Oberdorfer, Donald. *Electronic Christianity: Myth or Ministry*. Taylors Falls, MN.: John L. Brekke and Sons Publishers, 1982.

Ong, Walter, J. *The Presence of the Word: Some Prolegomena for Cultural and Religious History*. Minneapolis: University of Minnesota Press, 1981.

A Public Trust: The Report of the Carnegie Commission on the Future of Public Broadcasting. New York: Bantam Books, 1979. (Out of print.)

Schramm, Wilbur, and Porter, William E. *Men, Women, Messages and Media: Understanding Human Communication*. 2nd ed. New York: Harper and Row, 1982.

Schwartz, Tony. *The Responsive Chord*. New York: Doubleday, 1974.

Stephenson, William. *The Play Theory of Mass Communication*. Chicago: University of Chicago Press, 1967.

Wicklein, John. *Electronic Nightmare: The New Communications and Freedom*. New York: Viking, 1981.

Organizations

Action for Children's Television
46 Austin Street
Newtonville, Massachusetts 02160

American Council for Better Broadcasters
120 E. Wilson Street
Madison, Wisconsin 53703

Cable TV and Emerging Technologies Information Service
Communication Commission
National Council of Churches
Room 860
475 Riverside Drive
New York, New York 10115-0050

National Citizens Committee for Broadcasting
P.O. Box 12038
Washington, D.C. 20005

Telecommunications Consumer Coalition
105 Madison Avenue, 9th Floor
New York, New York 10016